UNDERSTANDING SOUND AND VIDEO RECORDING

by

MICHAEL OVERMAN

LUTTERWORTH PRESS · GUILDFORD AND LONDON

First published 1977

ISBN 0 7188 2285 4

Photoset and printed photolitho in Great Britain by
Ebenezer Baylis and Son Limited,
The Trinity Press, Worcester, and London

Contents

Introduction

The idea of recording music and singing for later performance must have been high among men's ambitions for many centuries. The world today would be inconceivably poorer without recorded music and speech, although it is only within the last hundred years that the dream has been realized. The true motivation for the earliest sound recording was its potential for office use. This was for recording speech, a 'talking machine' which could be used as an early Dictaphone.

Thomas Edison, the American inventor, is believed to have been the first person to have achieved practical success in this field when he produced a device which had some application to his work in telephony. It was after his first primitive speech recording machine had been built that his associate, Eldridge R. Johnson, who later founded the Victor Talking Machine Company, went to address an audience in Buffalo, New York State, on the invention. When the audience heard of the telephone talking machine, they reacted by enquiring whether it would be equally possible to record and reproduce music and song. It was this reaction that provided the impetus which gave rise to a remarkable new industry — the gramophone industry. In 1977 it celebrates the centenary of its birth. The other wonder of the age is, of course, video recording. It is now possible to put pictures of almost everything imaginable on tape and even on discs. My book tells how both these great events in human history have been achieved and explains how they work.

MICHAEL OVERMAN
Walkern, *May 31, 1977*

CHAPTER 1

Early Days

The ability to make music has been with man since earliest times. He achieved it first through the use of his own voice and with the aid of primitive percussion instruments. A time came when his inventiveness and ingenuity produced more sophisticated instruments, which enabled a performer to produce a variety of musical tones.

The music that man could by now make was richer in its variety, but the art of performance was more exacting, requiring a measure of technical as well as artistic ability. Time and determination were needed for a performer to develop the necessary skill. Nor was it easy either to build or acquire a musical instrument. So music making became a speciality confined to a small minority. Apart from the early equivalent of singing in the bath, the majority had to be content with listening.

The barrel organ
It was inevitable, therefore, that man began to develop new instruments which were easier to play and so quicker to learn. His mastery of mechanical skills was put to good use in the pursuit of this aim and a logical step was to invent an instrument which would produce music without the performer having to learn more than the simplest of mechanical actions. Thus was born the barrel organ — an instrument in which the music is preserved as a mechanical 'recording' which can be reproduced at will by an unskilled performer.

Barrel organs have a long and distinguished history. In 1597 Queen Elizabeth I commissioned a remarkable instrument to be made as a political gift for the Sultan of Turkey. Designed, built and assembled by organ-maker Thomas Dallam, it would play 'for the space of six hours together' and had several 'stops of pipes, viz, one open principal, unison recorder, octavo principal and a flute, besides a shaking stop, a drum and a nightingale'.

Though this is the first automatic organ of which we possess details, there is evidence of many earlier instruments. William of Malmesbury, a historian who died in 1142, describes a barrel organ built by Pope Sylvester II, when a young man, over a hundred years earlier, stating that it still existed at Rheims.

There is, indeed, a description of what would seem to be a primitive barrel organ in the writings of Ctesibius of Alexandria. Several authorities are of the opinion that the instrument described was in fact a self-playing organ and that it dates to the third century B.C.

Other automatic instruments were invented, too. Automatic carillons were built in the 14th century, automatic harpsichords in the 16th.

The early automatic organ, developed mainly to produce music for religious worship, was the forerunner of the more flamboyant fair ground organ. An oil painting made by Joseph Parry before his death in 1826 shows three small barrel organs in a fair ground scene — one slung round the neck of the organ grinder.

The musical box
The early 1800s also saw the development of another, much smaller, automatic music maker which, in due course, was to make it possible for ordinary people to enjoy music in their own homes without having to play an instrument or sing. This was the musical box, invented in Switzerland in the late 18th century. By 1815 a considerable industry was thriving at Geneva, where David Lecoultre soon established himself as a leading manufacturer.

The music box and the early barrel organ used the same system for 'recording' the music. The record was a drum studded with pins which operated the various notes (played by vibrating reeds) as it slowly rotated. Whereas the music box had a drum of metal on which the pins were permanently fixed, the organ had a wooden drum into which the pins and staples (used for sustained notes) were simply hammered. The drums of music boxes were generally permanent, but were built to produce a series of separate musical pieces, six or eight being typical. While each organ 'barrel' also accommodated six or more numbers, they were often interchangeable, and could even be returned to the factory to be stripped of their pins and staples and remade to produce new musical selections.

Fairground organs
By about 1870 automatic organs built specially for fairground use began to appear, the earliest of these being the so-called trumpet barrel organ, with its battery of brass trumpet-shaped resonators pointing forward from the reed assemblies that produced the strident music. It was designed to imitate a military band and was generally operated by a steam engine. The pioneer manufacturer of these organs was Gavioli of Italy, their operators becoming known as 'Gavimen'.

In 1892 Gavioli invented the 'book' organ, by then driven mostly by electricity, the current coming from a steam powered generator which could conveniently be situated some distance away so that its own noise would not disturb the music.

The book organ used an entirely new principle for recording — an endless band of card punched with holes. Folded zigzag to form a 'book', the card record could be of considerable length, was easy to manufacture and simple to store and to replace. Air was passed through the holes to actuate the notes.

The automatic mechanical organ reached the peak of its success about 1907 when fully chromatic models first became available. They were to survive for many years, though in the meantime a modest competitor, which was eventually to spell its eclipse, was beginning to exercise its muscles.

How elaborate these organs could be when fully developed is shown by the following list of stops of a typical organ manufactured by the Dutch firm of Mortier.

Melody (two octaves); Xylophone, Jazz flute; Vibratone, Violin (piano), Violin (forte), Trumpet, Saxophone, Unda maris.

Counter melody (one octave); Vox celeste, Saxophone, Flute, Cello, Bass cello.

Bass (one octave); Trombone.

Percussion: Cymbal, Bass drum, Side drum, Castanet, Triangle, Wood block.

Miscellaneous: Tremulant, Swell open, Swell shut, Declanche.

Until the arrival of the gramophone and, later, the radio

people were largely dependent for music on the public house
piano and the town band. The fair organ played a major part
in filling the need with a wide range of both classical and light
music, only turning to the 'pop' songs of the day when other
means of securing music became more widely available to the
general public.

The pianola

In 1904 a new system of reproducing music was successfully invented. This was the player-piano or pianola. Despite its being
limited to the piano, this remarkable machine deserves a few
words. Although the early models were no better than the
automatic organ in that they played piano compositions from
a punched paper roll without the need for a performer, they
were refined and developed into something quite unique — a
musical instrument which recorded and reproduced a pianist's
interpretation.

The master rolls were made by a punching system actuated
by the moving keys of an actual performance on a special
piano, and these holes faithfully reproduced the art of the performer as well as the composer's notes. The movement of the
pedals was included in the 'record' and each note played was
'measured' in terms of sixteen separate degrees of intensity and
recorded as such. So from the perforated rolls the pianola
reproduced not only the original notes, but their timing,
phrasing and 'attack'.

Like the book organ the player piano operated pneumati-
cally. Compressed air passing through the holes in the paper
rolls was used to operate the keys.

An interesting feature of the pianola was that composers
could, and sometimes did, write music for it that was beyond
the playing ability of one pair of hands. Such music had,
obviously, to be punched mechanically on to paper rolls and so
was not a recording in the modern sense.

The first talking machines

The work of some inventors is never translated into reality. So
it was in the case of Charles Cros (1842–1888) a French inventor who deposited detailed proposals for a 'talking
machine' with the French Academy of Sciences on April 10,
1877.

The American Thomas Alva Edison (1847–1931) is

generally credited with the invention of the first talking machine, which became known to the Americans as the phonograph. His first model could hardly be called a success, as the reproduced sound of speech was barely recognizable as words when it was first tested in July 1877. Edison set out to design an improved talking machine and completed his sketches in a notebook on November 29, 1877. The new machine was immediately built in his workshop by his mechanic, John Kruesi, and was completed and demonstrated on December 7 to the editor of the *Scientific American*. This 'tin foil phonograph', as he called it, recorded and played back intelligible speech. The first mechanically reproduced words, history tells us, were 'Mary had a little lamb'.

Edison's earlier unsuccessful instrument was designed to record on a paper tape impregnated with paraffin wax. Though it did not work, it was sound in principle. The instrument used a waxed paper tape on which a stylus, fixed to the diaphragm of one of Edison's early telephone receivers, cut an undulating furrow in the wax, the bumps corresponding to the vibrations of the diaphragm caused by a speaking voice. The paper was next drawn under a second spring mounted stylus fixed to another telephone diaphragm. In theory the bumpy furrow in the wax moved the stylus up and down, this in turn vibrating the diaphragm to reproduce the sound.

The successful tin foil phonograph was far more sophisticated. A brass drum about four inches in diameter was cut with a helical groove (as the thread on a bolt) on its outer surface running from one end to the other, the pitch of the groove being one tenth of an inch for each revolution. The drum was mounted on a threaded axle, the thread having the same pitch, so that one turn of the handle fixed at one end turned the drum through one circumference and moved it laterally the distance between successive grooves. The drum was covered with a sleeve of tin foil.

On one side of the drum was a recorder assembly consisting of a mouthpiece which concentrated a spoken voice on to a diaphragm fixed to a stylus which pressed on to the tin foil exactly over the groove in the drum. Vibration of the diaphragm produced sufficient pressure on the stylus to press the tin foil more or less into the groove, producing a firm furrow which undulated in step with the sound vibration. A repro-

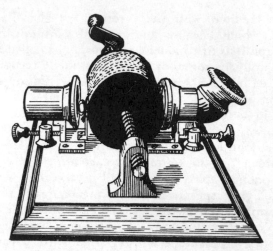

Fig. 1. Edison's tin foil phonograph, 1877

ducer, similar in design to the recorder, was mounted on the other side of the drum. When its stylus pressed lightly in the groove, while the drum was rotated at as near the original turning speed as possible, it reproduced the original sounds.

The indentations in the recorded furrow made by the tin foil phonograph were vertical, as in the case of the earlier waxed paper instrument, the furrow remaining straight in the direction of travel of the drum. This 'hill and dale' form of mechanical recording became known as 'phono-cut'.

Disc gramophone foreseen

Charles Cros's earlier invention was considerably more sophisticated than Edison's and foreshadowed the disc gramophone of later years. His proposal was to record on a smoke-blackened disc of transparent material, such as glass, using a stylus connected to a diaphragm so that it would vibrate laterally. The disc would rotate at a uniform speed, simultaneously moving slowly sideways so that the stylus would make a fine transparent spiral line on the smoked disc. When the stylus vibrated the line would undulate laterally. (The method was later called the 'needle-cut' system, to distinguish it from the 'phono-cut'.) The recorded disc would be used as a photographic negative to print on to a coating on a steel disc in order to produce an etched groove identical to the original spiral. The steel disc would be replayed by placing it on the

mechanism on which the glass disc had been recorded, allowing the stylus to follow the wavy furrow and so to vibrate the
diaphragm attached to it. This was undoubtedly a brilliant
idea for the times and it was unfortunate for Cros that he
failed to interest a manufacturer in his proposal.

The Phonautograph

While Charles Cros's invention, as described and deposited at
the French Academy of Sciences in April 1877, preceded
Edison's working tin foil phonograph by about 8 months, the
idea of recording sound was invented and carried out in
practice twenty years earlier, though no way of reproducing

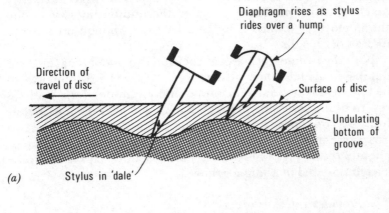

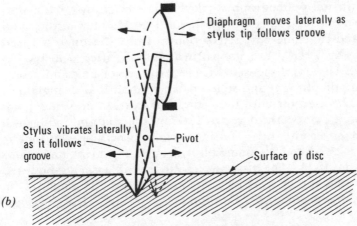

Fig. 2. (a) Principle of hill-and-dale recording;
(b) Principle of lateral cut recording

the recorded waves were proposed at that time. The recording machine, called the phonautograph by its French inventor Léon Scott de Martinville, was designed and first built in 1857 as a scientific instrument for the study of sound, and put on the market two years later by Koenig, a manufacturer of acoustic instruments.

De Martinville's invention had an open horn, about twelve inches long, as a sound collector, a diaphragm being fitted across its smaller end. A stylus fixed to the centre of this diaphragm scratched a helical track on smoke-blackened paper wrapped around a squat cylinder which rotated and moved laterally on a threaded axle in threaded bearings. This early machine thus produced a laterally undulating wavy line similar to that proposed by Charles Cros, though on a drum instead of on a disc.

Both the needle-cut (lateral cut) and the phono-cut (hill and dale) systems had their advantages. While the former was to be adopted as standard for mono (monophonic) discs, both 78 rev/min and long playing, the phono-cut method was sucessfully used on some early records, and a combination of the two was subsequently to prove more suitable for stereo (stereophonic) recording, where two separate sound tracks have to be accommodated in a single groove.

The Phonograph is improved
The tin foil phonograph worked well enough to warrant improvement, and since the quality of reproduction of the hand cranked machine suffered seriously from the uneven speed with which the drum was turned, Edison fitted a heavy flywheel. He also dispensed with separate recording and reproducing diaphragm and stylus pairs, finding that a single pair could be used for both functions. His third improvement was fitting a clockwork drive with a 'fan' mechanism acting as a speed governor and a falling weight providing the motive power. A tin foil phonograph with such a 'gravity' motor was built in 1878. The first successful use of a spring-powered clockwork motor to drive a phonograph was in England, in 1883, credit going to a London Schoolmaster, George Greenhill.

Alexander Graham Bell (1847–1922), inventor of the telephone, was naturally very interested in the newly invented phonograph. When he was awarded the French Government's Prix Volta for his own researches, the money was used to set up an organization to experiment in electro-acoustics. Some remarkable research was done. The technicians tried magnetic recording. They experimented with the transmission of sound to the recording diaphragm by means of a water jet. They tried using a jet of compressed air to 'read' the impressions of a recorded groove. They compared the 'hill and dale' method with 'lateral cut' recording. They tried recording on cylinders, discs and tapes.

Wax replaces foil
Finally, in 1885, they built their own 'talking machine' which they called the graphophone. Similar to the Edison phonograph in general layout, it recorded on a wax-coated cardboard cylinder. In many ways this proved more efficient than the tin foil sheet and the machine became the forerunner of the first generation of successful office dictating machines.

By 1888 Edison had adopted wax as the recording medium. But he used a solid hard wax cylinder and incorporated an 'erase' system — an automatic shaver which removed a thin layer of surface wax from a recorded cylinder, leaving it smooth and ready for use again. Both manufacturers now used 'hearing tubes' resembling those of a stethoscope. The Bell machine had an ingenious governor and operated from a treadle, while the Edison model incorporated an electric motor. This would appear to have been a great step forward, but we must remember that household electricity was yet to come; the energy source was an unwieldy 3-pint chromate cell with a working life of only 15 hours.

The era of the office dictaphone had now arrived and though manufacturers promoted their machines as suited to the recording of music, the quality of the reproduced sound needed considerable improvement before it could begin to compete with the automatic organ, the player piano and the music box as a means of taking music to the people. It did, of course, have one great inherent advantage. It not only recorded a performance, as opposed to a composition; it could record any instrument, any music and, in theory at least, even a full orchestra.

A new contender

While a commercial battle for the potential profits in the field of home entertainment began between the phonograph and the graphophone, an astute German who had emigrated to the United States from Hanover in 1870, and who had learnt the essentials of acoustics and electricity while employed by the Bell Telephone Company, visited the Smithsonian Institute in Washington and saw the phonautograph built in 1857, in France, by Léon Scott de Martinville. The German visitor to the museum was Emile Berliner (1851–1929) and his inventive mind was inspired by the old voice recording machine.

Berliner built himself a similar machine and, having produced a sound trace on smoked paper he 'fixed' it with a thin coat of shellac and set his mind to finding a method of converting this into a form which could be used to reproduce the sound. Whether or not in the course of his studies he came across Charles Cros's proposal is not known. He certainly used Cros's idea, for he arranged for a photo-engraver to reproduce his wavy line as an etched groove on a thin metal plate. Wrapping and fixing the plate around the drum of his machine it worked as a reproducer when the stylus was laid in the groove and the drum rotated.

Berliner realized at once that his system had one inherent fault. This was the fact that the recorded cylinder had to be cut and flattened out for the photo-engraving process and that the resulting etched plate then had to be made into a cylinder and joined up accurately (a difficult process) for replay. Emile Berliner solved this weakness by abandoning the drum and recording, instead, on a disc. He used a glass disc, coated on one side with a film of lamp-black mixed with linseed oil. He arranged that the stylus would track a spiral on the disc, as it rotated, and he fitted the disc with the coated surface down, so that the black material scratched off by the vibrating stylus would fall away and not clog the track. The flat disc could now be easily used to produce an etched metal disc for playback.

Berliner was not yet satisfied, as he considered the photo-engraving process to be too expensive for his ultimate purpose — the production of playable discs for a mass market. He set to work once more to find an alternative method. His solution was simple and effective. He replaced his glass disc with one of zinc, and he used beeswax dissolved in benzene in place of the lamp-black and oil. His stylus removed the wax as it tracked, exposing an even wavy line of metal. Chromic acid was now applied to the waxed surface of the disc which etched a groove that followed the recorded track.

Berliner had one problem remaining — that of reproducing the zinc 'masters' cheaply for the market. He solved this problem by means of a press and a hard plastic form of rubber. Each zinc master was first used to press a 'negative'. This, after hardening, was used in turn to press duplicate positives, again in hard rubber. Berliner was now satisfied. He called his new machine the 'gramophone' and demonstrated it before the Franklin Institute at Philadelphia on May 16, 1888.

Competition grows
Though the gramophone was on sale in Germany by 1889, marketed as a child's toy, it was not until 1893 that it entered the American market as a competitor to the already well-established phonograph and graphophone. Apart from the convenience of the flat record over the cylinder, Berliner, with his associate, Eldridge R. Johnson (1866–1945), the man who had earlier worked with Edison, was now able to sell cheap 7in. discs pressed in hard rubber from the zinc masters. On the other hand, the gramophone was only a player, while the earlier machines were recorders as well.

Berliner's gramophone also had a 'loudspeaker' in the form of a small metal horn, while the phonograph and graphophone, conceived partly as office dictating machines, still used 'hearing tubes' which were placed directly in the ears.

Within three years, a further major improvement was achieved; this was the replacement of the hard rubber disc by a shellac-based pressing — the material used for many years to make the popular 78 rev/min records, the manufacture of which was to survive until after World War Two.

By 1901 Johnson, who had formed his own company, the Victor Talking Machine Company, was manufacturing records using yet another process for preparing the masters. Instead of etching the groove on a zinc plate — a process which produced a somewhat noisy recording — Johnson cut the groove on to a hard wax plate. The surface was then made electrically conductive and a metallic coating deposited on it by electrolysis. When the deposit was thick enough the original wax was removed, leaving a strong metal negative which could be used directly for stamping shellac discs. Records made by this process had a better reproduction quality with a lower noise content, and the process was adopted in some form or other by virtually all record manufacturers.

While the quality of recording and reproduction was steadily improved the acoustic gramophone had one major disadvantage. As record making required the sound to be collected in a single horn which had, ideally, to be quite close to the sound source, the recording of anything other than solo instruments and singers, or of relatively small groups, presented a problem that could only be solved at the expense of balance, or overall quality, or both.

Horns, which varied greatly in design, had also replaced hearing tubes. While some early horns were flared at the open end, they were generally conical in shape, this being a simple form for manufacture. Though it was found by experiment that the horn's performance was improved by a measure of flare in its shape, it was not until 1919 that the theory of the exponential horn was published by the American scientist, Arthur Gordon. The principle of the exponential horn is that its cross section must double with each unit distance from the small end, the actual unit being arbitrary. The exponential horn was quickly adopted by gramophone manufacturers who found that it produced a distinctly improved sound, provided it was large enough. (A small exponential horn improves middle and high frequency reproduction at the expense of the bass).

The need for increased volume
The problem of increasing playback volume sufficiently for use in halls and even in the open air had been tackled much earlier. Of two ingenious early attempts, one used three horns playing simultaneously from three separate tracks on a single cylinder; the other had four horns playing from four discs on four turntables mounted one above the other on a single drive shaft. Both these inventions could have been used (though this was not their purpose) to produce stereophonic reproduction.

More successful was a system by which the vibration of the

reproducing stylus was made to modulate a supply of compressed air fed into the narrow end of an outsize horn. The system, perfected by Sir Charles Parsons and demonstrated to the Royal Society in 1904, worked well enough for it to be used later to present concerts in London's huge Albert Hall. It was also used successfully in many hotels, restaurants and public parks, and to provide the sound for early talking films.

Markets flooded

In 1906 Eldridge Johnson's Victor Talking Machine Company had put on the market the first phonograph which had its horn hidden within its cabinet. He called it the Victrola, and with it he started a fashion which was to change the image of the industry, only seven years after the Gramophone Company of London had bought the famous painting by Francis Barraud that was to immortalize the old horn gramophone in the famous 'His Master's Voice' trade mark.

After the appearance of the first Victrola the markets of Europe and the United States were flooded with a remarkable variety of phonographs, graphophones and gramophones, as more and more manufacturers entered the business with all manner of variations designed, not always successfully, to get round the patents held by Edison, Bell, Berliner and their associates. Cylinders persisted until 1913 but the 10in. and 12in. 78 rev/min double-sided shellac disc, pioneered by the British Gramophone Company, eventually superseded them.

Meanwhile the gramophone was steadily improved and a wide range of models introduced. There were portables, drawing room models, budget models, concert models. There were models with large horns, small horns, fancy horns, plain horns, exaggerated horns and concealed horns.

Two radical improvements were simple and yet important enough to be widely adopted. One was the introduction of the 'tone arm', the other of the expendable steel needle.

Originally the stylus and reproducing diaphragm was connected rigidly to the horn. As the former had to track the recording, the entire horn had to be suspended so that it could swing, most of its weight being carried by the support. The tone arm however was a device which connected the reproducing head to the horn by means of a tube having one vertical and one horizontal pivot. The former allowed the head

Fig. 3. A typical phonograph of the 1908 period

assembly to track the record, while the latter ensured that only the weight of the head itself, and not the entire tone arm and horn, was supported by the record. With this device it became possible to build a fixed horn of any suitable shape. It made possible the design of concealed horn gramophones, ranging from the popular portable — the shape and size of a small suitcase — to cabinet models styled as pieces of fine furniture.

The system of providing an expendable steel needle had two advantages. Formerly the stylus would become so worn with use that it would cause damage to the grooves of a record. By discarding a worn needle (which was simply fitted into a hole and fixed there by tightening a screw with a milled head like a watch winder) and replacing it with a new one, groove damage by a worn stylus was avoided. And by substituting a thin or thick needle for a standard needle, the volume of the reproduced sound could be made softer or louder.

CHAPTER 2

Electronics Takes Over

Enrico Caruso had made recordings in Milan as early as 1902, and some other eminent opera singers had followed his example. But if the early records of those days served to preserve voices that would otherwise never have been heard by later generations, they could hardly do justice to musical groups, let alone to the symphony orchestra. By 1917 Leopold Stokowski had been persuaded to conduct the Philadelphia Orchestra in the cramped Victor recording studio — a panelled room with the large end of a metal horn, like a huge ear trumpet two feet across, projecting from a small hatch in one wall, about 5ft from the floor. His early recordings (such as the famous Hungarian Dance No 5 and the equally well-known Minuet by Boccherini) received great praise from the early critics. But when Arturo Toscanini, touring the United States with an Italian orchestra, made some trial acoustic recordings in 1920 he was dissatisfied with the result and refused to sign a contract.

The problem that faced the early makers of musical recordings lay in the fact that the acoustic (non-electrical) method collected and applied the sound to the diaphragm of the recording machine without amplification. The recording horn concentrated the sound, but that sound had to be produced quite close to its mouth if sufficient movement of the cutting stylus was to be induced. Another difficulty was that the system was more sensitive to middle and high frequency sound than to bass vibrations, and recordings were to that extent unsatisfactory, even when bass instruments (such as the 'cello) were doubled with bassoons or tubas to exaggerate their tone.

The microphone had been invented in 1876 (it was part of the earliest telephone equipment built by Alexander Bell), and had since been refined and improved. The idea of using a number of microphones to pick up the sound from the various sections of an orchestra, and of combining their outputs electrically, was attractive. But the electrical output of the microphone was, at best, very low, and there was at first no method of using this low output to actuate a recording stylus.

The vibration of the early telephone receiver diaphragm was inadequate.

The electronic amplifier

In 1907, the American scientist Lee de Forest invented the triode valve. This was an electronic device which could be connected in a circuit so that a low alternating voltage, applied to its control 'grid', could be made to influence the passage of an electric current between the valve's 'cathode' and 'anode'. The varying output current could in turn be used to produce a greatly magnified alternating voltage which followed the variations in the control voltage fairly accurately. In other words the triode valve was the basis of an electronic amplifier. The output of a microphone — or for that matter the outputs of several microphones, mixed together — could now be amplified.

While the microphone, the amplifier and the loudspeaker were developed by the radio industry the electro-mechanical groove cutter had to be designed specially for sound recording. Work on developing a cutter had begun by 1915, but the war intervened and it was not until the early 1920s that practical equipment was produced.

The electric disc cutter

The monophonic disc cutter was generally what is known as a dynamic transducer, operating somewhat in the fashion of a dynamic (or moving coil) loudspeaker, only in place of the loudspeaker cone it had a cutting stylus fixed to the vibrating 'voice' coil.

It worked well and achieved an enormous improvement in the quality of recorded sound. Even with the somewhat primitive acoustic gramophone of the time, reproduced music now had a more natural tonal quality.

The introduction of the loudspeaker by the radio industry had brought home to the gramophone manufacturers the inadequacy of the acoustic gramophone's sound quality. They realized that in due course the buying public would recognize the superiority of the radio's sound, and that gramophone and record sales would suffer unless improvements were made. A magnetic pick-up was soon invented so that records could not only be made with electronic aid, but could also be played

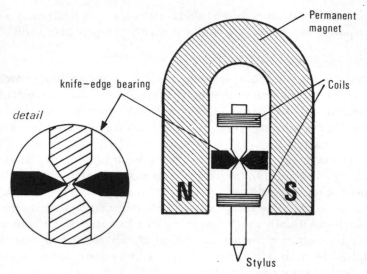

Fig. 4. *Principle of early moving-coil disc-cutting head*

electrically. But the improved acoustic gramophone was selling well. The leading manufacturer — the American Victor Company — believed that a change to electric gramophone manufacture, and the consequent introduction in the factory of an entirely new technology, would have put up the cost of gramophones beyond the reach of those who were then buying.

The gramophone is improved

So Victor's took the decision to improve, rather than run down the acoustic gramophone, and one of the results was the 'Orthophonic Victrola'. Research had shown that a relationship existed between the length of a horn, its rate of taper and the size of its mouth. To do justice to the improved new electrical recordings a horn had to be truly exponential in shape, and at least nine feet (3 metres) long. The Orthophonic Victrola had just such a horn, suitably folded and partially divided, within its floor-standing cabinet.

The result was outstanding. The perceived frequency range of electrical recordings played back on the Orthophonic Victrola now extended from 100 to 5,000 cycles per second, almost $2\frac{1}{2}$ octaves more than on older equipment. Bass response was superior to that of the early loudspeaker radio.

The production of records
Record manufacture soon became a standardized process employing the microphone, the amplifier and the electro-mechanical disc-cutter, along with an improved version of Berliner's stamping technique and Johnson's system of making metal masters.

The original master was cut directly on to a blank disc consisting of an aluminium base (for strength) coated with a cellulose lacquer. It had been found that a very clean groove could be cut in cellulose using a hard polished chisel-shaped stylus, which was usually made from sapphire or ruby. The blank was fixed to a heavy turntable driven by an electric motor designed to maintain speed accurately whatever the resistance caused by the groove cutting process.

The cutter was made to track, as the blank turned, by being mounted on a long screw of suitable pitch, fixed so that as it rotated the cutter moved slowly along a radius of the turning blank. The stylus removed a continuous thread of cellulose as it cut the groove, and a simple suction tube was fitted to carry this away so that it could not foul the process.

The system described so far produced a simple spiral groove, V-shaped in cross-section, which usually started near the outer edge of the blank. (Some early records were cut starting near the centre.) And as soon as a suitable alternating current was fed into the voice coil assembly on which the stylus was mounted, the stylus vibrated laterally as it cut, producing a wavy instead of a straight groove.

As a rough surfaced groove produced a fine hissing sound on playback, smoothness was an important factor in reducing the background noise of a recording. While a well polished stylus produced a reasonably smooth surfaced groove, it was found that the smoothness could be improved by heating the stylus. This was achieved by incorporating a tiny coil of high resistance wire around the shank of the stylus, the coil being fed with low voltage direct current.

In most of the standardized 78 rev/min records used almost universally for two decades the spiral groove was cut at a pitch of 96 to the inch (some manufacturers used a finer pitch at times) the typical triangular groove being 0.006in. wide at the top and 0.0025in. deep, with a slightly rounded bottom.

Mass production

It was possible to play back from a cellulose master disc, but the material was relatively soft and even the lightest stylus would cause wear to the groove. Repeated playings would quickly result in irreparable damage. For this reason masters were never used for playback. Instead they were used to make a master negative which, in turn, could be used to press a large number of copies in the shellac composition then used.

The negative, or matrix as it was called, was prepared by first dusting the positive master with fine bronze or graphite powder so that the surface would conduct electricity. The treated master was then immersed in an electroplating bath so that a thin copper or nickel deposit was built up on its surface. When thick enough, and so strong enough, the metal deposit was separated from the master. ·

The metal negative could now be used in a hydraulic press to stamp out copies of the original master, using heat supplied by steam circulated through the press platens to soften the shellac blanks, followed by cold water to harden the pressing before the press was opened.

As a metal matrix would only produce about 200 pressings before a deterioration in quality became discernible, a three step process was introduced. Under this system the negative metal matrix was used to prepare a metal positive, known as a 'mother'. The mother, being much less susceptible to damage than the original cellulose master, was then used to make a large number of duplicate metal negatives, known as 'stampers'. Each stamper could then be used to make up to 200 high quality pressings on shellac or, in later years, on vinylite blanks. Vinylite (a man-made resin) was to replace shellac (a natural resin) because it produced considerably less surface noise and had a much higher resistance to breakage.

Six years after Toscanini had tried and rejected acoustic recording as unsatisfactory, he was persuaded to visit the recording studios once more to see whether electrical recording would satisfy him where acoustic recording had not. It was in 1926 that he conducted the New York Philharmonic Orchestra in a performance of the Nocturne and Scherzo from

Mendelssohn's 'Midsummer Night's Dream'. The result was still not up to the standard he demanded and it was not until 1929 that he began to make records regularly. By then, the superiority of electrical reproduction, as well as of the recording process, had been established.

The gramophone pick-up

Electrical reproduction was based on another device designed specially for the purpose. Known as the pick-up, the earliest models simply replaced the acoustic sound box, using the same expendable steel needle which was held in a metal collar by a hand-tightened grub screw. No heavier than the old sound box and tone arm it replaced, the early pick-up was straight, with a double hinge at the far end. This hinge permitted vertical movement, so that the head could be raised to change the record and to change the needle, and horizontal movement so that the head could follow the groove and track the record.

The purpose of an electric pick-up is to convert the physical movement of the stylus into a corresponding electrical signal. The motion of the stylus is a vibration which corresponds to the recorded sound waves. The pick-up must produce an electrical signal which faithfully follows the frequency and amplitude variations of the vibrating stylus, and so of the recorded sound.

Just as an alternating electric current in a coil of wire produces a changing magnetic field through and around that coil, the opposite is also true. If a coil of wire is situated within a moving magnetic field (and provided the wire of the coil is connected to a continuous electric circuit), an electric current is induced in the wire and it varies in frequency and amplitude in step with the changes of direction and intensity of the magnetic field.

This is the principle used in the electric generator, which achieves the movement of the magnetic field across the windings of its coils in one of two ways. Either the coils are fixed and a magnet is made to revolve inside or around them; or the magnet is fixed (which makes a larger, more powerful magnet possible) and the coils are mounted on an axle so that they revolve between the magnet's poles.

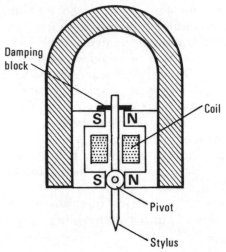

Fig. 5. *Principle of early moving armature magnetic pick-up*

Types of magnetic pick-up

The magnetic pick-up can also be designed to work in either way. The 'moving armature' pick-up, has a length of soft iron cantilevered so that its free end, which carries a stylus, can vibrate between the north and south poles of a 'folded' permanent magnet. The armature also passes through a tiny fixed coil. When the armature vibrates the metal disturbs the magnet's natural field, and the disturbances, duplicated in and around the armature, induced tiny voltage changes in the wire of the coil.

A variation is found in the 'variable reluctance' pick-up. In this case the metal that supports the stylus extends the magnetic circuit from one pole of the permanent magnet; a divided metal yoke extends the magnetic circuit from the other pole, and is fixed so that the armature vibrates within the two branches of the magnet's opposite pole. A pair of coils are wound around the arms of the yoke. When the armature vibrates the magnetic field of the system is disturbed, inducing voltage changes in the windings of the coils.

When a typical moving armature pick-up follows a 1,000 Hz record track with an amplitude of 0.0254mm (0.001in.), the output voltage averages 0.01 volts.

A little more sophisticated than the two types we have described is the moving-coil, or 'dynamic' pick-up. This design incorporates a coil which is pivoted so that it can move bodily, in step with the vibration of the stylus to which it is connected. Mounted around one pole of a folded permanent magnet and within the other pole (which is concentrated around a hole in the metal) the coil, by vibrating within the most concentrated part of the magnet's external field, induces changing voltages within itself. The output of the dynamic pick-up is less than that of the moving armature types. A recorded waveform of a 1,000 Hz sound with an amplitude of 0.0254mm (0.001in.) produces, in a typical dynamic pick-up, an output of about 0.001 volts.

We can see now that electrical reproduction may be thought of as the opposite of electrical recording. The latter process comprises:

A. The microphone, which converts the physical energy of sound waves into corresponding electrical waves.
B. The amplifier which multiplies the tiny output voltages of the microphone, and delivers corresponding waves of electrical power.
C. The disc-cutter, which converts the electrical output of the amplifier into corresponding physical movement of the cutting stylus, which in turn 'stores' the sound waves in the form of a wavy groove on the record disc.

The electric 'gramophone' consists of:

A. The pick-up which converts the physical movement of the reproducing stylus as it follows the groove of a record, into corresponding electrical waves.
B. The amplifier which, again, multiplies the tiny output voltages of the pick-up, and delivers corresponding waves of electrical power.
C. The loudspeaker, which converts the electrical output of the amplifier into corresponding physical movement of the loudspeaker cone, which in turn produces sound waves.

Electronics takes over
The year of change was 1925. In April the Victor company released the first electrical recording to be put on public sale.

It was a trial production and was sold in Philadelphia only. In May the company issued the first disc to be offered for sale in record shops throughout the United States. This was a popular foxtrot: 'Let it Rain, Let it Pour' played by Meyer Davis and his Le Paradis Band. By June it was available in England, too. In June Victor released the first 12in. electrical recording of two classics, Chopin's 'Impromptu in F major' and Schubert's 'Litany' played by the pianist Alfred Cortot. The same month Columbia put on sale a 12in. electrical recording of 'John Peel', sung by 850 voices on the stage of the Metropolitan Opera House, New York, and 'Adeste Fideles' sung by the choir and audience, totalling some 4,850 people. And in July Victor released the first electrical recording of a symphony orchestra. Leopold Stokowski conducted the Philadelphia Orchestra in 'Danse Macabre' by Saint-Saëns.

With the appearance of improved recordings came the need for improved reproduction. Victor's excellent Orthophonic Victrola was in the shops by November and a month later Brunswick set the pattern for years to come when they put the first all electric phonograph on the market. They called it the Panatrope.

That year of change ended with yet another landmark, this time in Britain, where His Master's Voice released the first electrically recorded full symphony, Tchaikovsky's Fourth, played by the Royal Albert Hall Orchestra under Sir Landon Ronald.

CHAPTER 3

In Pursuit of Fidelity

We have already seen how the early electrical recordings offended Toscanini's ear. To understand why we must find out how they differed from the first so-called 'high fidelity' recordings of the mid-thirties, and from the first microgroove LP recordings of 1948. The principal differences (apart from the obvious mechanical ones) fall into four separate areas. These concern:

    A. Background noise
    B. Frequency range
    C. Loudness or dynamic range
    D. Length of continuous play

Noise
While noise may include many frequencies, its main peculiarity is that it has no harmonic structure.

When a stylus tracks an unmodulated groove (one without wave form), there should, in theory, be no reproduced sound. In fact a fine high pitched hiss is produced by the friction, however slight, between the stylus tip and the sides of the groove along which it runs. When loud enough to be audible this constitutes noise. (An amplifier also produces electrical noise — again a slight hiss. But this is normally insignificant.)

The old acoustic gramophone did not produce too much audible hiss as its output of sound at high frequencies was low. This is why the old shellac 78 rev/min discs sound so much more noisy on the modern electric gramophone. The modern machine amplifies the surface noise that the old gramophone conveniently suppressed. The use of a polished and heated recording stylus reduced this inherent noise, and when steel needles were replaced by the modern, polished, reproducing stylus of sapphire or diamond, the natural hiss was further reduced. Finally it was virtually eliminated when, in 1948, shellac was replaced by vynilite as the material from which discs were pressed.

In assessing the noise of a recording we speak of the signal-to-noise ratio. On a gramophone record this is simply the ratio of the loudness of the noise to that of the loudest recorded sound, the latter being limited by the space available for adjacent grooves to follow the wave-form without breaking into each other. More precisely, the signal-to-noise ratio is defined as the difference in decibels between the loudness of the noise and that of sound produced by a 400 Hz tone recorded at the maximum possible amplitude.

For those that understand mathematics a decibel (dB) is one tenth of a bel (B), which is the logarithm to the base 10 of the ratio between the intensity of two sounds. This seems complicated, but it is a logical scale because when the pressure of a sound wave on the human eardrum is doubled, the increase in perceived sound level is too small to be recognizable. The ear's perception of loudness follows an approximately logarithmic scale. So a logarithmic unit of loudness makes sense. In fact the smallest increase in loudness which the average ear can notice is around 3 dB. An increase of 10 dB sounds twice as loud to the ear.

The range of the decibel scale is shown by the following examples. If the threshold of hearing is rated as zero decibels, an average whisper at 5ft (1.5m) will have a 'loudness' of about 10dB. By contrast the loudness of a typical conversation will be 50 dB, that of a symphony orchestra averaging about 75 dB and of a large aircraft passing low overhead 100 dB. Perceived loudness reaches the 'threshold of pain' at between 130 and 140 dB.

A signal-to-noise ratio of 50 dB is the minimum acceptable in a modern sound reproduction system, though in early days a ratio of 35 dB or even less was normal. Toscanini would have heard considerable needle hiss in those early recordings — too much for his sensitive ears.

Frequency range

The concept of frequency range is easy to understand. The lowest note of an 88 key piano is A, with a fundamental frequency of 27.5 Hz. Middle C has a frequency of 261.63 Hz, the A above it (which is the reference note for concert pitch tuning) has a frequency of exactly 440 Hz, and the top note, C (four octaves above middle C) has a frequency of 4,180 Hz. While the fundamental frequencies are those I have given, musical notes normally include harmonics and the sound of a piano includes a significant proportion of harmonics up to something over 7,000 Hz. Some other instruments produce higher harmonics; for example, the significant harmonics of the violin extend up to about 12,000 Hz.

The old lac gramophone record could not reproduce nearly so wide a range of frequencies. Its sound output was fairly good over the four octaves from a frequency of about 200 Hz (about the G below middle C) to about 1,500 Hz (the third G above middle C). Below 200 Hz the output fell away rapidly, producing a recording that lacked greatly in bass. Above 1,500 Hz the tones could be heard, though the output fell away quickly and most of the important overtones which characterize the timbre of the various instruments were totally absent.

The invention of electrical recording resulted in a great improvement in frequency range. The first electrically recorded discs were capable of a reasonably good sound output from about 100 Hz (an octave lower than before) up to 5,000 Hz (a little over one and a half octaves higher). Played back on an Orthophonic Victrola or a Panatrope electric gramophone the listener could now hear previously unrecorded bass frequencies which gave recorded music added body, and he could begin to hear high overtones, which made the sound of the various instruments much more realistic.

By 1948, when the term 'high-fidelity' had suddenly become important to a discerning section of the listening public, the effective frequency range of quality recordings had been extended down to about 50 Hz and up to 10,000 Hz, adding another octave at each end of the recorded sound spectrum. Now, with well-designed play-back equipment, it was possible to reproduce an orchestra with a sound that was remarkably like the real thing. Most of the lowest bass frequencies and most of the important overtones were within the recorded range and could be reproduced with quality equipment.

In the process of widening the frequency range a new problem had arisen, however.

We saw in the previous chapter how the magnetic pick-up acts as a miniature generator. This generator produces a tiny output voltage which varies according to the speed at which the vibrating stylus moves. There are two factors which govern this speed of movement. The two pairs of grooves shown in Fig. 6 illustrate these two factors.

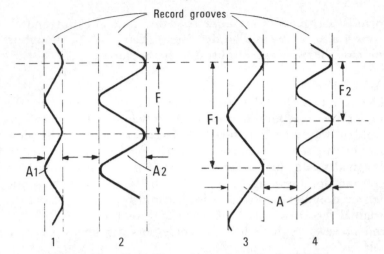

Fig. 6. The effect of frequency and amplitude variations

Tracks 1 and 2 show two sounds of the same frequency (the distance F between two peaks in the waveform is the same) but of different loudness (the amplitude A of track 2 is greater than that of track 1). In the case of tracks 3 and 4 the amplitude of the two waves is the same, but the frequencies F1 and F2 of the two waveforms are different.

When a stylus tracks these grooves the pick-up head is virtually stationary and it is the grooves that move along. It is not hard to see that a stylus following tracks 1 or 2 will vibrate at the same frequency, but because the sideways movement in track 2 is greater, the stylus will have to move from side to side at a faster rate in track 2, in order to follow the longer path of each wave in the same period of time. The sideways velocity of the stylus thus varies according to the amplitude of the wave. So the louder the reproduced sound the greater the stylus velocity. In the second pair of tracks the amplitude of the waves is the same. But in this case a stylus in track 4 has further to travel because it has to move from side to side twice as often, in the same period of time, as a stylus following track 3. In this case the higher the frequency of the reproduced sound the greater the stylus velocity.

As the voltage produced by a vibrating stylus varies in step with the stylus velocity, we are faced with an anomaly. Track 2 produces a higher voltage, and so a louder sound than track 1, which is fine, because the increased amplitude of the waveform is the result of a louder recorded sound. Unfortunately track 4 also produces a louder sound than track 3, though in this case the two wave amplitudes are the same.

Constant velocity
The result is that the higher the recorded frequency, the louder the reproduced sound. An obvious solution to this problem would be to reduce the electrical output of the pick-up for higher frequencies. An electronic circuit can be designed to do this so accurately that the result would be a 'constant loudness' signal, in which the loudness of the sound delivered by the loudspeaker is the same as the loudness of the original recorded sound, however high or low the frequency, and however high or low the corresponding pick-up output voltage.

An alternative solution would be to doctor the input voltage to the recording head when the master is being cut, so that the amplitude of the wave falls with increasing frequency, thus keeping the effective stylus velocity constant for sounds of equal loudness at all frequencies.

Constant amplitude
The second alternative would appear to be more practical as electric gramophone circuits would be simpler. But in this case another problem arises. Because of the constant velocity characteristic, the wave amplitude of a recorded track would be greater (for any given loudness) the lower the frequency. This means that very loud low notes would produce a waveform of considerable amplitude.

To accommodate such occasional loud low notes adjacent grooves of a recording would have to be set slightly further apart than the greatest possible wave amplitude. Otherwise the peaks of the waves of adjacent grooves might foul each other. By setting the grooves this far apart a great deal of disc surface space would be wasted because even where some loud low notes do occur, most of the recording would be at a significantly lower amplitude.

To avoid wastage and provide longer playing time on a record, the electronics are devised so that frequencies below 1,000 Hz are recorded at constant amplitude. This means that all low frequency notes have the same amplitude of groove

wave for a given loudness. On playback the pick-up output
voltage will now rise with frequency up to 1,000 Hz, and to
compensate for this an electronic circuit is introduced between
the pick-up and the amplifier. This process of correcting the
output is called equalization.

Constant amplitude is not only useful in providing increased
record playing time by reducing the amplitude of the groove
wave at low frequencies. It is also used to improve the signal-
to-noise ratio at high frequencies. This is achieved in the
following way.

Dynamic range
An important feature of orchestral music is the enormous
range of loudness of which it is capable. A full orchestra will
frequently produce a volume of 75–100 dB above the
threshold of hearing, and a large orchestra occasionally
reaches a loudness of as much as 120 dB above the threshold of
hearing. On the other hand an orchestra can play down to a
pianissimo of only 20 dB — little more than the sound of a
whisper.

The dynamic range of the orchestra is thus commonly 80 dB
and may be as high as 100 dB or more. This enormous
dynamic range cannot easily be reproduced on a gramophone
record because loudness is limited by the distance between
grooves (since this in turn limits the amplitude of the wave)
and softness is limited by the noise of the stylus in the groove
(which remains constant as the output of sound is lowered).

Groove noise is more apparent at high frequencies, because
the stylus must move along the rapidly undulating groove at a
much higher velocity than when following a low frequency
wave. On the other hand the increase in velocity at high frequencies is compensated during constant velocity recording, as
we have seen, by a reduced wave amplitude, so that the output
of the magnetic cartridge will produce a constant loudness as
the frequency reproduced rises.

Since high frequencies would thus normally be recorded at
relatively lower amplitudes, there is room on the disc to exaggerate these amplitudes. By doing this, and by incorporating
an equalizing circuit in the player to reduce the reproduced
volume of high frequencies until they are back to normal, as it
were, the groove noise is simultaneously reduced in volume.

The result is an increased signal-to-noise ratio. This was not done in the mid 'twenties.

RIAA[1] characteristic
It is now clear that in the making of recordings there are advantages in reducing the amplitude of low frequencies, and in increasing that of high frequencies. It would seem logical, therefore, to incorporate circuits in the recording amplifier, to produce a constant wave amplitude for sounds of equal loudness at all frequencies. In practice the required rise in velocity to achieve constant amplitude is equal to 6 dB per octave. With average good recordings having a frequency range of rather over 8 octaves, from about 40 Hz to 12,000 Hz, the velocity variation would have to be equal to 48 dB to achieve constant amplitude. This was an unduly high figure when the recording characteristic was standardized internationally in 1953. A compromise was achieved by approaching constant amplitude below about 1,000 Hz and above about 2,000 Hz, keeping constant velocity between these frequencies. The resulting curve thus had a 6 dB/octave slope in the lower and higher frequencies, where this was most desirable, while the overall increase from end to end was only 4 dB/octave, thus reducing the velocity range to a comfortable 32 dB within the 8 octave range.

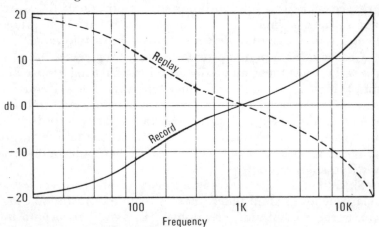

Fig. 7. RIAA Record/Replay Characteristic for long-playing discs

[1] Recording Industry Association of America.

All disc recordings today are made to comply with this curve, and all magnetic pick-ups are followed by an equalizing circuit which converts the rising output below 1,000 Hz and above 2,000 Hz back to a constant figure.

The crystal pick-up

Long ago, in 1880, the Curie brothers, conducting electrical research at the Sorbonne in Paris, had discovered that when crystals of Rochelle Salt are twisted a voltage is generated across them. Known as the piezoelectric effect, this phenomenon was put to work in the crystal pick-up. This is a simple device. A sandwich is made of two thin flat crystals, with metal foil between. One end of the sandwich is held in a tiny clamp attached to a bar to which the stylus is fitted. The other ends of the two crystals each has a foil connection on the outside of the sandwich, all being held in place by a fixed rubber clamp. When the stylus vibrates, causing twisting of the salt slabs, a voltage is generated across the two outer foil connections. Where the recorded groove waveform has an amplitude of 0.001in., a typical output voltage of 0.5 volts is produced — very considerably more than that generated by any magnetic pick-up.

The Rochelle salt crystal is somewhat brittle, and a modern variation of the piezoelectric pick-up uses ceramic slabs in place of the salt. Though the voltage output is not quite so high, the principle is the same.

There is another significant difference between the magnetic and the crystal pick-up. While the voltage output of the magnetic pick-up varies with the velocity of the stylus vibrations, in the case of the crystal it varies with their amplitude. In other words the further you twist a Rochelle salt crystal or ceramic slab, the higher the voltage produced. The speed at which you twist does not affect the output. How does this effect the problems of equalization?

We have seen that records are made with constant amplitude at low frequencies (to make possible an increased dynamic range), and also at high frequencies (to improve the signal-to-noise ratio). This treatment results in sounds of constant loudness producing a rising voltage output as frequency is increased. The magnetic pick-up produces an increasing loudness as the voltage rises, and so the equalizing circuit is designed to cut the loudness as the frequency grows higher, producing a final output of unchanging loudness. We have also seen that crystal and ceramic pick-ups do not give added loudness with increased frequency. They respond only to changes in amplitude. As the recording characteristic produces a constant amplitude groove wave for sounds of constant loudness, the crystal and ceramic pick-up will give a constant loudness output without any equalization. We have seen that the RIAA recording curve is not a continuous straight line, easing off in the middle to a short stretch recorded at constant velocity (and so varying amplitude). Over this portion of the sound spectrum, crystal and ceramic pick-ups will give a rising output with increasing amplitude. But this portion of the curve is so short that it does not seriously impair the apparent overall sound output of the piezoelectric pick-up.

Playing time
We have already discussed three problems which may have contributed to Toscanini's dissatisfaction in 1920. Apart from excessive groove noise, inadequate frequency range, and limited dynamic range, there was another cause for discontent. This was the relatively short playing time of the disc. Improvements had been made. The early cylinders would give a playing time of only about two minutes. This was then extended, by using larger cylinders, to a maximum of four minutes. The early 10 inch 78 rev/min discs played for about $2\frac{3}{4}$ minutes, but the 12 inch records introduced in 1903, would play for 4 minutes with standard groove spacing, and up to 6 minutes when the groove spacing was reduced — possible in music which included no very loud passages. The introduction of the electrical player, and the device of equalization which made the constant amplitude recording a practical possibility, made feasible the 6 minute, 12 in. disc even with loud orchestral music. Toscanini could still not record a complete symphonic movement on a 12in. disc, let alone a whole symphony, but it was at this point in development, when both frequency and dynamic range had been increased and noise reduced that he agreed to record regularly.

Subsequently, of course, came the microgroove record, in two forms. The 45 rev/min 'extended play', and the $33\frac{1}{3}$ rev/min 'long playing' disc competed for popularity for a time. The latter ultimately became the standard for major orchestral and other long works, with its potential of 25 minutes playing time in the 12in. size. The 45 rev/min gained the advantage for shorter pieces and became the accepted cheap high-fidelity disc for popular music in the 7in. size.

Record Changers

Before the introduction of microgroove recordings, manufacturers found a ready market for automatic record changers. Many ingenious mechanisms became available to allow one to play a stack of discs without having to touch the record player. Some machines could handle a stack of mixed 10in. and 12in. discs. Some could even turn a record over. The most popular mechanisms played one side only of each disc, and to suit this system record manufacturers issued long works in two forms — normal and with 'auto' coupling. In the latter version, instead of side 2 of a piece of music being stamped on the reverse of side 1, side 4 on the reverse side of 3 and so on, the first half of the entire work would be found in sequence on different discs, the other half on their backs. In a work covering six sides, side 6 would be found on the back of side 1, side 5 on the back of side 2 and side 4 on the back of side 3. In this way the three records could be stacked on a record changer and the stack needed turning over only once, half way through the work.

Dual stylus pick-ups

When the EP and LP disc was introduced manufacturers were faced with the problem of producing players which would accommodate both the existing 78s and the new microgroove recordings. The standardized stylus for 78 rev/min records had an effective tip diameter of 0.003in., while for microgroove recordings a tip diameter of 0.001in. was adopted. This meant that if a pick-up was to be used with both types of record, there had to be two styluses. The solution to the problem lay in the introduction of a new kind of pick-up head, incorporating quickly changeable twin styluses. Unfortunately this type of dual cartridge presented design problems which prevented its development as a genuine high-fidelity device. The enthusiast who desired the best in Hi-Fi reproduction had to settle for microgroove reproduction only.

Tracking error

The pursuit of high-fidelity led to a number of improvements which were independent of the change to microgroove recording.

It is not difficult to appreciate that a pick-up head should track the record with its transverse axis exactly at right angles to the groove (Fig. 8).

Diagram A shows clearly that the head of a straight pick-up, pivoted at one end, traces a circular course across the disc, and that its transverse axis will therefore be at an exact right angle to the grooves at one point only. This problem of 'tracking error' was minimized by a simple geometrical expedient — that of having the head at an angle to the arm, as in diagram B. A pick-up can be designed on this principle so that tracking error is all but eliminated.

Stylus tip shape

The shape of the stylus tip is important for several reasons. The groove cut during recording is 'V' shaped and the replay stylus is designed so that it is supported by the sides of the groove, but does not reach its bottom where dust inevitably collects. In this way the noise which would be caused by a sharp tip running along in the dust is avoided. The area of contact between the rounded stylus tip and the groove sides is also naturally small, again reducing noise. But the less the area of contact the greater the actual pressure between stylus and groove; so to reduce the risk of damage to the very rapid undulations of a high frequency wave form, the modern stylus

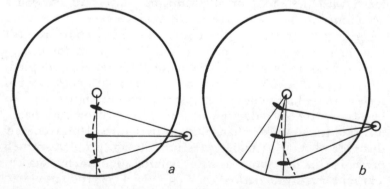

Fig. 8. The correction of tracking error

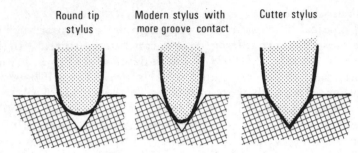

Fig. 9. Stylus shapes

has a short portion which is more conical than rounded.

The recording cutter, looked at from above, is chisel shaped, with the result that the groove width varies slightly, being greatest at the peaks of each wave. This variation, known as the pinch effect, means that a round stylus will ride up very slightly at the narrow part of the groove, and will fall very slightly at the peaks. This vertical movement can cause distortion in playback and can even cause needle chatter. To avoid this the elliptical stylus was introduced. As its long dimension remains across the groove, like the long dimension of the cutter that made it, it more accurately follows the path of the original cutter, and avoids any vertical movement due to the pinch effect (Fig. 10).

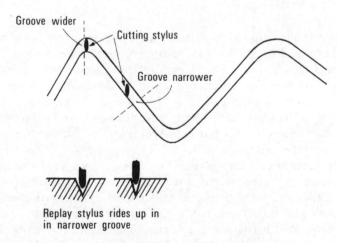

Groove wider

Cutting stylus

Groove narrower

Replay stylus rides up in
in narrower groove

Fig. 10. Pinch effect

A Physical Problem

The physical dimensions of a record groove are important in many respects. The microgroove became standardized with a width, at the top, of 0.0025in. and a depth of 0.0013in. With a disc speed of $33\frac{1}{3}$ rev/min a 10 kHz waveform will have a recorded wavelength of about 0.003in. at the outside of a 12in. disc, reducing to 0.0015 at the inside. The maximum amplitude is generally restricted to about 0.005in. So even at the outside the stylus tip, when reproducing the higher harmonics which are so important in high-fidelity, has to follow a zig-zag path which moves it up to 5 thousandths of an inch from side to side more than 300 times in each inch of groove. On the inside of the disc this last figure is doubled. The speed of change in direction of the stylus is at times so great that truly enormous acceleration is required as the stylus tip rounds the extremes of a wave (where the lateral movement is momentarily nil) and moves off in the opposite direction. If you measure the pressure of the side of the groove on the stylus tip at the moment of maximum acceleration it will be found, in the case of loud high harmonics, to reach as high as 1,000G (that is 1,000 times the pull of the Earth's gravity at sea level).

In order that such enormous pressure should not damage the groove it is essential that the vibrating stylus tip should have the minimum possible resistance to movement; or in technical language, the minimum mechanical impedance.

The Cartridge

The early pick-up, with its steel needle, had a relatively high mechanical impedance, so engineers set to work to design pick-up heads (or cartridges, as the removable assembly became known) in which the stylus could move much more freely. Mechanical impedance, they found, is caused by three factors: effective tip mass, compliance, and damping. Together they define what is conveniently called the 'tracking ability' of the cartridge.

Tip mass affects impedance because the greater the mass of an object the greater the force required to accelerate that mass. This can be most easily understood in terms of momentum. A cannon ball requires a much greater force than a small bullet, to give it the same velocity. The tip of the stylus acts like a minute projectile being thrown from side to side by the pressure of the wall of the oscillating groove. The lighter its effective tip mass the less the force needed to slow it down and change its direction of travel.

Compliance and Damping

The tip of a stylus cannot move as freely as a bullet because it is part of the stylus which, in turn, is fixed to the armature of the cartridge. The freedom of movement of the stylus tip is thus reduced by the stiffness of the assembly, and it is a measure of this stiffness which we call the compliance. When the stiffness is such that a force of one dyne causes a deflection of one millionth of a centimetre, the compliance is said to be 1cu (one *compliance unit*).

Ideally stiffness should be as low as possible, and so compliance as high as possible. In practice a compliance of 5cu is sufficient for a stylus tracking at 1 g (total effective weight on the groove) to follow a groove at the generally accepted maximum amplitude of 0.005 cm. With higher tracking weights the compliance can be lower.

But a high compliance will leave the armature free to move too near the magnetic pole pieces within which it is designed to vibrate and generate current. This causes trouble because the strength of the magnetic field varies with the distance from the poles. To prevent this some form of mechanical damping is incorporated in the mount which holds the armature, and this damping reduces the natural compliance.

Tip Mass

We have already seen that the effective tip mass must be low. Figures as low as 1 mg (one thousandth of a gram) are achieved today. This figure, of course, has nothing to do with the weight of the stylus, or with tracking weight, though the latter is certainly related to it because the greater the effective tip mass, the greater the tracking weight needed to ensure that the stylus faithfully follows the groove. Without going deeply into mathematics we can estimate effective tip mass by the following equation:

$$M = 10T \div 6.25$$

where M is the effective tip mass in milligrams and T is the tracking weight in grams. This rule of thumb assumes a fre-

quency of 10 kHz and a stylus velocity of 10 cm/S, both
generally used as standards for this purpose.

Turntable noise
As the modern cartridge is extremely sensitive it not only
produces a signal corresponding to the groove undulations on
the disc, but can respond to any vibrations that may be transmitted through the turntable. This type of unwanted response
is the cause of 'rumble'.

Rumble was unimportant in early days as its frequency is
generally very low — around 20 Hz is typical — and the early
amplifiers produced little output at such low frequencies. The
coming of 'high-fidelity' amplifiers changed this and made
rumble a real problem.

There are two main sources of rumble: vibration from the
turntable motor, and vibration from the turntable's own bearing. Designers reduced the former by mounting the motor on
rubber or composition supports, and by driving the turntable
either through a rubber or composition idler wheel, or by
means of a rubber or composition belt. The latter system,
which is more costly, is the more effective. Turntable bearing
noise was minimized by eliminating the ball race and support-
ing the turntable shaft on a single well lubricated steel ball.

The automatic record changer was particularly prone to
rumble and with the arrival of microgroove recording, with its
greatly increased playing time, manufacturers found the
reduced demand did not warrant the design of mechanisms
which produced less turntable vibration. So the automatic
changer has become obsolescent and mechanisms of this kind
are today only made for the juke box.

Turntable speed
It is obviously essential, if the pitch of recorded music is to be
identical, on playback, with that of the original, that the
speed of the recording and playback turntables should be the
same. Turntable speed must therefore be accurately controlled, and the adjustable governor of early days has given
way to the synchronous electric motor in which the frequency
of the alternating current which powers it is used to control its
speed. It is then no problem to devise gearing to relate the
motor speed to the 45 or 33⅓ rev/min of the turntable. It is of

interest to note that, unless you are a musician with the gift of perfect pitch, small inaccuracies in turntable speed have little noticeable effect. An error of as much as 6 per cent in turntable speed alters the pitch of reproduced sound by about one semitone — too little for most of us to notice unless we check with a tuning fork or a piano.

A simple speed check can be made using a stroboscopic disc. This has a series of evenly spaced short thick black lines or bars round its periphery. It is placed on the turntable and lit by a fluorescent or neon lamp which, unseen by the eye, gives a light output which varies in step with the alternating voltage of the mains. For the 50 Hz A.C. we have in Britain, the stroboscopic disc to check a turntable speed of $33\frac{1}{3}$ rev/min must have 180 circumferential bars. When spinning at exactly $33\frac{1}{3}$ rev/min in a 50 Hz fluorescent light the bars appear to remain still. If the bars seem to be revolving slowly clockwise the turntable is running fast; if anti-clockwise the turntable speed is slow. A stroboscopic disc to check a 45 rev/min turntable speed should have 133 bars.

More important, because the ear is sensitive to a lack of steadiness in pitch, is the inability of a turntable to maintain a perfect steady speed. Cyclic speed changes of this nature produce pitch variations which we call 'wow' and 'flutter'. The former term is used for pitch 'wobble' having a frequency of less than 5 Hz (usually much less); flutter is the name given to the same effect occurring above 5 Hz.

Wow and flutter can be effectively minimized by the use of a heavy turntable running on a good single ball bearing.

Equalization

Once we have converted the mechanical signal of the recorded groove into an electrical equivalent with the correct frequency, an absence of wow and flutter, and a low signal-to-noise ratio, we have to modify it so that the constant velocity sections of the recorded frequency range are converted back to the loudness values of the original sound; then we have to amplify it and feed it to one or more loudspeakers in order to convert the electrical signal into equivalent sound waves.

The processes of equalization and amplification are carried out in the record player's pre-amplifier and amplifier — both usually built into a single unit.

Equalization is achieved by passing the output signal of the cartridge through a network of resistors and capacitors. In the case of a magnetic cartridge this network is so designed to boost the base and treble portions of the signal to the exact extent to which they were reduced while recording to the standard RIAA curve.

Because the voltage output of a magnetic cartridge is low, and the equalization network further attenuates the signal, the equalizer circuit is followed by an amplifier stage. Next the signal is passed through a tone control network which, on all true high-fidelity equipment, includes a treble boost and cut control, and a separate bass boost and cut control. When these are both set at their central zero position, the output should be normal and correct, and the main purpose of these controls is to tailor the sound to the listener's personal preference. When naturally loud music is played fairly softly, for example, the bass response appears to the ear to be less than the response at high frequencies. To compensate the bass can be suitably boosted by turning up the bass tone control. Indeed most good preamplifiers have a 'loudness' switch. This is intended for use when normally loud music is played relatively softly. When switched on the loudness control provides bass boost automatically.

As we have already seen crystal and ceramic cartridges operate in such a way that they automatically equalize an RIAA recording with a fair degree of accuracy throughout the frequency range. For this reason a crystal or ceramic cartridge is not connected to the magnetic cartridge input of a pre-amplifier. Indeed, as they give a greater voltage output than magnetic cartridges, they are normally connected to bypass both the equalization network and the first amplification stage. Their output is fed straight into the tone control network.

The signal from the tone control stage is passed to a volume control (also called a gain control), which feeds the preamplifier's second amplification stage. It is the output of this stage that is fed to the main amplifier.

The purpose of the main amplifier is to convert the output signal of the pre-amplifier into a form which will drive one or more loudspeakers. It must achieve this with a 'level' response over a wide frequency range and without introducing any electrical noise which might impair the wanted sound generated by the loudspeaker system.

A good high-fidelity amplifier should have a level response within two decibels, from about 20 Hz up to 20 kHz. The amplifier's signal-to-noise ratio should be not less than 60 dB, and harmonic distortion (the electronic generation of spurious harmonics) should not exceed one per cent.

Loudspeakers

And so we reach the final link in the chain — the loudspeaker system which converts the amplified electrical signal into sound waves.

When an orchestra plays, the vibrations of the air which bring the sound to one's ears come from a host of different sources. To produce the sound of a single loud chord there may be 20 or 30 vibrating violin strings, as well as those of several violas, cellos and basses, plus a variety of notes from woodwind, brass and percussion instruments.

That the human ear can distinguish between so many simultaneous vibrations may seem remarkable. In fact nature has designed the ear extremely cleverly, giving it a separate resonating 'hair' for each and every frequency in the audio spectrum, each tuned hair having a separate nerve connection to the brain. If a piano has 88 notes with 88 separate tuned strings (many of them in pairs of threes), the ear has many thousands of tuned hairs. It is as though each ear contained several thousand tiny microphones, each tuned to a separate frequency, each connected to a master mixing unit in the brain.

If it seems remarkable that the ear can discriminate between the myriad sounds of an orchestra playing, how much more remarkable it is that a microphone, with a single membrane to resonate to the complex sound waves (or perhaps a group of half a dozen microphones), can produce a single electrical wave pattern which can be converted into a single record groove which will carry all the information necessary to define the music. How remarkable, too, that we can reconvert that wavy groove into an electrical signal which faithfully duplicates the output of the microphones used to make the recording. And finally, how amazing that a stiff paper or composition cone, the cone of a loudspeaker which may be only a few inches in diameter, can be made to vibrate by that electrical signal so that it will produce sound which seems to the human ear to be remarkably similar to that produced by the many instruments of the orchestra all playing together.

In point of fact the modern microphone — or a group of microphones — can produce an electrical signal which corresponds so faithfully to the combined waveform of the original sound that we call it *high fidelity*. That signal can be recorded and reproduced and amplified with very little loss in its original fidelity. When it comes to the loudspeaker we find it is virtually impossible to design a single unit which will give the correct output of all parts of the audio spectrum. An 8in. or even a 6in. diameter cone can effectively produce sound waves between about 200 Hz and 10,000 Hz. But the reproduction of music requires a bass range at least down to 40 Hz, preferably lower, and of overtones at least up to 15,000 Hz, preferably higher.

There have been two approaches to this problem. One has been the design of special wide-range loudspeakers incorporating two separate sound radiators, one for the low and the other for the high frequencies. This type of loudspeaker can be efficient but is expensive. The other approach uses two or three separate units for different parts of the frequency range. The great advantage of this system is that the high frequency radiator does not have to stand up to the high powered vibrations of the low notes. The amplifier output is divided by an electronic network so that only the frequencies required pass into the voice coil of each separate loudspeaker. As most of the power goes into the bass, this means that high frequency units can be much smaller and more efficient.

The most popular high-fidelity loudspeaker system uses three units. The bass radiator, known as the 'woofer' is usually either 12in. or 15in. in diameter; the mid-range unit, called the 'squawker', is conveniently of 6in. or 8in. size. The high frequency loudspeaker, the 'tweeter', is perhaps 3in. in diameter.

The Cross-over Network
The amplifier output is passed through a simple network of capacitors and inductances which allows frequencies up to about 2 kHz to the bass circuit, those between 2 kHz and 5 kHz

to the mid-range terminals, and those above 5 kHz to the high frequency circuit. The cut-off between each circuit is not abrupt, but is designed to roll off gradually so that there is a suitable overlap. Hence the name 'cross-over'. The cross-over frequencies given above are not rigid. Some loudspeakers may give better results with higher or lower cross-overs. Nor is it essential to have three loudspeakers with two cross-overs. Two loudspeakers with a single cross-over are a common alternative.

In order that even a 12in. loudspeaker should produce a good bass response, the back and the front of the cone must be acoustically isolated. Ideally the unit should be fitted over a hole in a wall, so that sound waves from the front cannot mix with those from the back — some of which may partially cancel the others out. This is because a sound wave is a wave of alternating pressure in the air. If a high pressure peak of a wave from the back of a loudspeaker cone arrives at the front in time to meet the low pressure trough of the corresponding wave from the front, the high and low pressures will obviously tend to cancel each other. The two waves, each representing an identical sound, are said to be out of phase. In practice loudspeakers are mounted in enclosures which provide a suitably long path between front and back. Many wave peaks and troughs may still coincide, but they will not be the peaks and troughs of the identical original sound.

Some early loudspeaker enclosures were 'horn-loaded', which meant that the unit was fitted at the narrow end of a folded exponential horn, somewhat like the 'orthophonic' gramophone horn. Research has found alternative enclosure designs which provide an excellent result without the enormous bulk of the horn. The theory of these enclosures is somewhat complex, but those who wish to study it will find numerous practical books of reference.

One other point is worth noting. Bass waves radiate naturally in every direction, while high frequency sounds tend to follow a straight line at right angles to the vibrating loudspeaker cone. To distribute sound more generally it is therefore necessary to design a system to deflect the sound from the tweeter. Various methods are used. One is to provide a reflector which 'bounces' the high frequency waves into a wider radiation pattern. Another is to use a wide-flared horn on the tweeter.

Impedance Matching

You cannot connect any loudspeaker to any amplifier. In the first place a unit must be capable of handling the maximum output of an amplifier without distortion. So if an amplifier is rated at 12 watts output, the loudspeaker must be rated at 12 watts or more. The loudspeaker must also 'match' the impedance of the amplifier output, which is usually between 3 and 16 ohms. If you connect a 4-ohm loudspeaker to a 16-ohm amplifier output the amplifier may deliver too much power, may overheat the output stage and may damage the loudspeaker. A 16-ohm loudspeaker driven from a 4-ohm amplifier output will reduce the amplifier's power output significantly. In either case the mismatch may cause distortion not present in the original signal. Ideally the loudspeaker and amplifier impedance should match exactly. In practice a difference of a few ohms is acceptable. Indeed the impedance of a loudspeaker system varies with the frequency of the output. This is why modern loudspeakers are often rated with a bracketed impedance: for example 3–6 ohms or 6–12 ohms.

The loudspeakers one sees in the Hi-Fi shop look disarmingly simple. Usually they are in the form of a tall rectangular box with a broad-weave fabric covering the front. Cheap loudspeakers of this form may contain one simple unit. The more expensive ones hide two or three separate units with their built-in cross-over networks.

CHAPTER 4

Sound from Around

At first sight it would seem logical that a stereophonic system should sound more realistic than the old single-channel gramophone. Because we have two ears, one on each side of the head, we can judge the direction from which sound is coming. We can distinguish between a live orchestra and recorded orchestral music from a loudspeaker, because the sound of the former reaches us from different directions, while that from the loudspeakers does not. The purpose of stereophonic sound systems is to feed different 'versions' of each sound to each ear and so simulate the original more accurately.

Deceiving the Ear

While the logic is clear the problem of reproducing the real thing is not so simple. The sound that reaches a listener's two ears can certainly be separately and accurately recorded by placing a pair of directional microphones facing away from each other, about nine inches apart, like a pair of ears. The sound picked up by each microphone can be simultaneously but separately recorded and simultaneously but separately reproduced. By using a pair of earphones the sound picked up by the left microphone can be fed into the left earphone, and so only into the left ear; and the sound from the right microphone only into the right ear.

But the moment you use loudspeakers instead of earphones the two channels of sound are no longer isolated. Now sound from the left loudspeaker reaches both ears, as does sound from the right loudspeaker; and the ear is often smart enough to recognize that there are in fact two separate sound sources, and that there is no sound coming from any other direction.

Experimenters found that it was possible to deceive the ears by recording the two channels by means of microphones placed well apart (as are the loudspeakers in a stereophonic reproducing system.) In this way sounds from the left are picked up much more strongly by the left-side microphone, those from the right are picked up more strongly by that on the right, and sounds from the middle are picked up equally by each microphone. Careful placing of microphones and loudspeakers can thus give a remarkable sense of presence and sound from around. Unfortunately the position of the listener in respect to the two loudspeakers is critical. The two loud-speakers must be the right distance apart, must not be too near the side walls of the listening room, and must be roughly equidistant from the listener. The actual geometry of their placement will be discussed later.

Two Problems
Once research had established that a stereophonic system could achieve added realism in sound reproduction, two problems had to be solved.

The first was to find a practical and economic system for recording and reproducing two simultaneous channels. The second was to manufacture stereophonic records and repro-ducing equipment and persuade the public to buy them.

The Need for Compatability
There would clearly be market resistance to any new system. Enthusiasts with record collections and high-fidelity mono-players would not wish to discard these. Nor would they buy stereophonic recordings which they could not play on their existing players. From a commercial point of view the only practical way of making the change was therefore to evolve a system which was compatible, in as many respects as possible, with the old. The solution was as simple as it was clever. The first step for the enthusiast who wished to make the change was to replace his pick-up cartridge (a relatively small item) with a new stereo cartridge. This could be fitted to the existing record player, would play mono records through the mono amplifier, and would also play stereo records through the mono amplifier. Now the owner could buy all new recordings in stereo.

The next step would be either to duplicate the existing mono amplifier, so as to have two identical sets, for a stereo amplifier is simply a pair of mono amplifiers (each including its preamplifier). Now stereo records could be played to pro-duce stereo sound, while the old mono records could still be played in mono, the same sound being produced by the loud-speaker system of each set. Those purchasing new stereo equipment would also know that they could play earlier mono recordings through them if they wished.

The Standardized System

The 'compatible' stereo system that became standardized carries the two sound tracks in a V-shaped groove almost identical with the old mono L.P. groove. Instead of the groove undulating sideways, each wall of the groove now undulated at right angles to its surface; so one wall carried one sound channel, the other the second channel. The new stereo cartridge was designed so that the armature carrying the stylus could vibrate separately in response to undulations on each wall of the groove, vibration in the two directions producing separate signal currents in two separate coils.

It is interesting here to note that this system was neither the old hill-and-dale cut of the early cylinder phonograph, nor the lateral cut that had become standard for mono discs. Instead it used two cuts at right angles to each other, each at 45° to the surface of the record. Even more interesting is the fact that when an identical sound is recorded in each channel the groove shape will cause a stylus to vibrate vertically as it tracks, without moving from side to side. So a mono signal recorded on a stereo recording system produces a hill-and-dale cut,

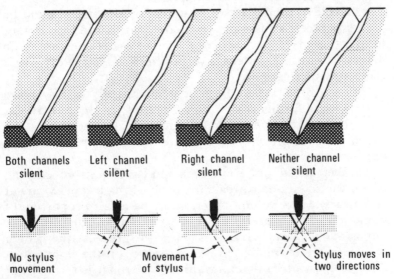

Both channels   Left channel   Right channel   Neither channel
    silent   silent   silent   silent

No stylus   Movement   Stylus moves in
movement   of stylus   two directions

Fig. 11. The stereo groove

while the old mono systems produces a lateral cut. Compatability was achieved by producing a cartridge in which the stylus could vibrate either laterally or vertically (or in any combination of the two) producing two electrical outputs which, combined, would form a mono signal, or which could be fed separately to two amplifier and loudspeaker systems to produce a stereophonic result.

The Stereo Amplifier
In practice the two amplifiers (each including a preamplifier with identical equalization, tone and gain control circuits) are built as a single matched pair. Often, too, a 'balance' control is incorporated. This is designed to raise the gain of one amplifier as it lowers that of the other. In its central position the gain of each should be the same. The purpose of the balance control is to compensate for variations in the apparent output of each channel due to the positioning of the loudspeakers in a room, the shape of the room and its furnishing, and their relationship to the listener.

Loudspeaker Placing
As the frequency response of loudspeakers varies, it is important that a pair of stereo loudspeakers should be identical or 'matched' in respect of sound quality.

As a rule of thumb a pair of stereo loudspeakers should be placed between 3 and 4 metres apart, and should face inward so that their axes meet between 3 and 4 metres in front. The diagram illustrates alternative positions in a typical living room 4 × 6 metres in size.

Unless a room is very large it is not usually wise to place loudspeakers further apart than 4 metres, as the human ear tends to lose the 'stereo image' and instead detects that the sound is arriving from two separate sources with an acoustic gap between them.

To keep the sound from each loudspeaker from echoing round the room and so reaching each of the listener's ears at very nearly equal volume, there must be a fair proportion of sound absorbent materials within the room. In particular it is important to avoid parallel echoing surfaces. As the ceiling and floor are normally parallel, a carpet on the floor (or at least on most of it) is important. If the room is rectangular some sound absorbent material on one end and one side wall is

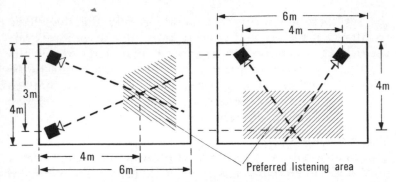

Fig. 12. Loudspeaker placement

also advisable. Thick curtains across most of a window wall will take care of one pair of parallel walls, and soft upholstered sofas and chairs with some soft wall hangings will damp any reverberation between the other two walls.

Loudspeakers should preferably be placed about a metre off the floor, so that their horizontal axis is at about the height of the seated listener's ears.

With rooms of unusual shape or proportions experiment is necessary. Provided the general principles explained for the typical rectangular room are remembered, it should not be too difficult to find the best position to create a good stereo image. Remember that the image will vary with the position of the listener, and in some rooms it may be difficult to accommodate more than three easy chairs from each of which a satisfying stereo image can be heard.

Reverberation
We have stressed the importance of avoiding unwanted echoes in a listening room. All echoes could, in theory, be eliminated by fixing sound-absorbent materials on ceiling, floor and all four walls. The result, however, would be sound which could only be described as 'lifeless'. All natural sound includes a proportion of continuing echo, and variations in this proportion gives sound a quality of 'brightness' which is hard to define though easy to recognize. The word 'continuing' is important here. Single echoes are clear-cut and produce a confusion of sound, especially when they repeat, as in a typical swimming pool. A 'continuing' echo, known as reverberation, results in the gradual fading away of each separate sound.

The sound of an organ and choir in a church is enriched by

the reverberation within the building, and the shape and treatment of the walls of concert halls are chosen to provide the richness which the listener expects. For a large orchestra a reverberation time (the time taken for a single sound to die away to inaudibility) of between 1 and 2 seconds is not too much. For a small orchestra one second is enough. For pop music a half second is usually better.

Quadraphonic Sound

To produce natural reverberation of even one second with a normal sound reproducing system would need a listening room as large as a small concert hall. This is why sound engineers have been experimenting for some years with 'quadraphonic' sound. The principle is simple. By having four separate sound channels it should be possible to present the listener with not only a good stereo image of the direct sound, but also with a good stereo image of the reverberation present in a concert hall.

It would seem possible to achieve this with a conventional stereo system. A pair of microphones used for recording an orchestra will not only pick up the direct sound, but also the reverberating sound arriving from the back of the concert hall. The snag is that when reproduced the reverberation will reach the listener from the same loudspeaker as the direct sound, while in a concert hall the reverberations come from anywhere but the same direction. Quadraphonic recording therefore uses directional microphones, suitably placed, so that the minimum of the reverberating sound is picked up by the main microphones, and the minimum of the direct sound by the second pair of microphones, which are intended to pick up the reverberation.

Once sound has thus been separated into four channels it can be reproduced through four amplifiers and four loud-speakers to produce an acoustic image which will give the listener a very realistic impression of presence in a concert hall.

The Problem of Compatability

This theory had engaged the inventiveness of engineers for some years. As we shall see in the next section of this book recording on magnetic tape provided a simple practical means of achieving quadraphonic reproduction and by 1961 a quadraphonic tape recorder was available in the United States. But the majority of high-fidelity enthusiasts preferred discs and engineers were faced with the challenge of inventing a system which would be compatible with the existing standard stereo reproducing equipment. To expect the owners of expensive stereo units to scrap them in favour of new quadraphonic sets was out of the question. If quadraphonics were ever to gain popularity two conditions were essential and a third desirable. It must be possible to upgrade a stereo system to reproduce quadraphonic recordings, and it must be possible to play stereo recordings on quadraphonic equipment. If possible it should also be possible to play a quadraphonic disc on existing stereo equipment to produce acceptable stereo sound.

These three objectives, it seemed to engineers, could only be achieved by a system which somehow compressed four channels into two during the recording process and sorted out the two channel information to produce four again for reproduction. This 4-2-4 system, as it came to be called, had the potential advantage that the system that had been developed to carry the two channels of stereo radio broadcasts on a single FM (Frequency Modulation) transmission; it could presumably be used to broadcast the two-channel intermediate stage of a quadraphonic recording without modification. The two channels delivered by the FM radio receiver could then be fed into a quadraphonic record player to produce quadraphonic sound in the home.

The Matrix System
A practical solution to the problem was not evolved until 1969. It was Peter Scheiber, an engineer-cum-musician, who announced the relatively simple 'matrix' system. The approach was to feed four channels into an electronic circuit which produced a two-channel output. This output could be recorded by conventional equipment on an L.P. disc which, in turn, could be played back on conventional equipment. The two-channel output could then be passed into a matrix similar to that used for recording, to produce a four-channel output. The Scheiber matrix is, in effect, a simple amplifier bridge circuit.

At first sight this circuit would appear to be too simple. The

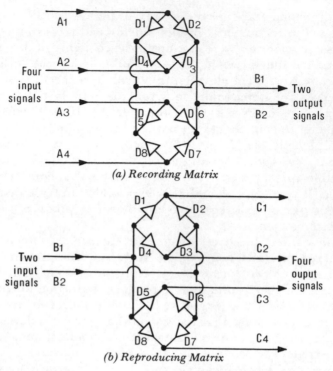

(a) Recording Matrix

(b) Reproducing Matrix

Fig. 13. Quadraphonics: 4-2-4 Matrix System

four recording signals A1–A4 would surely become so mixed as to produce two similar if not identical outputs, B1 and B2. The outputs would, in fact, be identical if the eight matrix amplifiers D1–D8 all operated in phase at the same level of gain. By altering these a wide variety of mixtures of signals A1–A4 can be achieved in signals B1 and B2. And by operating the reproducing matrix amplifiers at corresponding phase and gain differences, four signals C1–C4 can be produced which are similar to the original signals A1–A4. The word 'similar' is significant. There is always a proportion of cross-talk which cannot be eliminated.

The Scheiber system achieved two essential conditions of compatability, but not the third. A 4-2-4 recording, made with the matrix system, would not produce true stereo sound on existing stereo equipment. It could, however, be played on existing stereo equipment, without using a matrix, to produce an acceptable, if 'diluted' stereo image of the original. This, reasoned many manufacturers — especially most of those in Japan — would be good enough for the enthusiast who wished to upgrade his existing stereo system. He could either convert by adding a matrix unit and a pair of additional amplifiers and loudspeakers; or he could purchase a complete new quadraphonic unit. In either case his existing collection of stereo records could still be played. He could also make the change gradually, buying and playing quadraphonic recordings on his existing equipment, and only upgrading and changing the latter when he considered his collection of the new recordings was sufficient to warrant the expense.

The 4-2-4 matrix system came on the market during 1969–1970 under many names such as 'SQ' (Sony), 'QSC' (Sanyo), 'QS' (Sansui), 'Ambiphonic' (Hitachi), 'X-1' (Onkyo) and 'Quadrilizer' (Pioneer).

An Alternative System

Despite its relative simplicity, the 4-2-4 matrix system was not a true four-channel system because, as I have already said, inter-channel crosstalk could not be fully eliminated. This fact encouraged several major manufacturers to think again. A solution was soon found by using an existing telephone technique. Telephone conversations are 'stacked' on long distance lines, enabling many calls to be made without crosstalk, over each pair of conductors. This is achieved by a technique borrowed from yet another technology — that of radio. For radio transmission the audio signal is first superimposed on a high frequency 'carrier' wave, in the process known as modulation. At the receiving end, after selecting the wanted carrier from the thousands broadcast by means of a resonant tuning system, the received signal is demodulated to produce the original audio signal without the high frequency carrier.

In the case of the long distance telephone, carrier waves are similarly modulated with speech signals. Modulated carrier waves of different frequencies, if spaced at a separation at least twice that of the highest audio frequency being used, can be transmitted along the same cable. They need to be separated by tuning at the receiving end, and finally demodulated to produce a series of quite separate audio signals.

This technique, in a simplified form, is the basis of the CD–4 quadraphonic system pioneered by JVC/Nivico in Japan

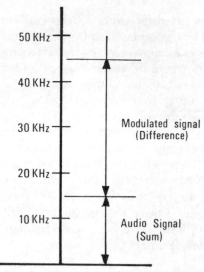

Fig. 14. Quadraphonics: CD4 frequency distribution

(JVC stands for Japan Victor Company) and quickly adopted by their associated American company, RCA, and several others.

In CD–4 (which stands for 'Compatible Discrete 4-Channel') two of the four channels are recorded as normal audio signals with a frequency range of 30 Hz–15,000 Hz. The other two audio channels are each frequency-modulated (this is a standard process on FM radio) on to a 30 Hz carrier wave, producing two signals varying in frequency from 15,000–45,000 Hz. Each FM signal can now be added to one of the audio signals to produce a combined signal covering a frequency range of 30 Hz–45,000 Hz, without any over-lapping.

It might be assumed that the normal left and right 'front' sound signals would be recorded on the two audio channels of a CD–4 set, the reverberation (or 'rear') signals being modulated to occupy the higher frequencies. In fact the standard adopted by the record companies is more subtle. If we call the two 'front' signals FL and FR and the two 'echo' signals EL and ER, the technique is to first add the two left and two right signals. FL + EL, and FR + ER are used as the basic stereo pair in the audio spectrum. The audio pair thus includes both the front and rear components of the original sound so as to give the best stereo image on standard stereo replay equipment.

The signals which are frequency modulated on to carriers are the difference signals FL — EL, and FR — ER. These signals, being generally of lower amplitude, can be more conveniently modulated and recorded.

When a CD–4 record is played back on normal stereo equipment the difference signal (assuming that the stylus can follow the high frequency undulations in the groove) cannot be heard as the human ear cannot hear sound above about 15,000 Hz.

In a CD–4 replay unit, however, the modulated signals are first separated by frequency filters and demodulated by normal FM techniques. Next the four signals (FL + EL), (FR + ER), (FL — EL) and (FR — ER) are electronically processed (not a difficult problem for the design engineer) to produce four new signals, FL, FR, EL and ER, corresponding to the original sound with no crosstalk. All that is then necessary is amplification of the signals and delivery to suitably placed loudspeakers.

The CD–4 system clearly has an advantage over 4-2-4 in that it avoids crosstalk. It also has disadvantages.

Many mid-fi cartridges will not track accurately much above 20,000 kH. This is not serious as the first step in upgrading an existing stereo player for CD–4 is to change the cartridge. There are a number of existing cartridges that will track at the required high frequency, though it has been found that a modified stylus (basically elliptical) may be necessary in some cases. A CD–4 recording should never be played back using a mid-fi cartridge as the FM part of the groove wave will probably be damaged. Indeed any cartridge operating at above 2 grams should not be used.

Once the right cartridge is in use a CD–4 recording is fully compatible. It not only can give a high quality stereo output on a normal stereo player, but can also produce an excellent result in mono.

Quadraphonics by Radio

When it comes to transmission by radio, CD–4 is at a serious disadvantage. The bandwidth of a radio wave is twice the maximum frequency transmitted, half above and half below the carrier frequency. In practice, world-wide authorities have allotted radio channels for public broadcasting with band-widths of 9kHz in some cases and 10kHz in others. This means that the audio frequency transmitted must not exceed 4,500 Hz and 5,000 Hz respectively. This is satisfactory for music broadcasts in mono or stereo because although it necessitates cutting the higher frequencies of high-fidelity audio signals, 4,500 Hz is high enough to give a reasonably good mid-fidelity result. Clearly, though, if a CD–4 quadraphonic recording is played in a radio studio, the electronic circuits which limit the frequencies in order to keep the radio signal within the permitted bandwidth will cut out the high frequency modulated difference signals altogether. The resulting radio wave can be received and played back in stereo by a conventional stereo receiver, but quadraphonic reproduction is impossible.

In the case of the 4-2-4 system there is no such problem. The two-channel 'mixture' of the original four recorded signals lies entirely within the normal audio spectrum, and limitation to 4,500 Hz or 5,000 Hz will affect only the fidelity of the signals in the same way as occurs with normal stereo recordings. The stereo pair can be transmitted and received in the usual way and then either reproduced in stereo or matrix-processed to produce the four signals needed for quadraphonic reproduction.

Re-recording on Tape
The same limitation applies to CD–4 when it comes to recording on magnetic tape. As we shall see in Chapter 6 even the best tape-recorders marketed for normal sound recording are not designed to recorded frequencies above 20,000 Hz, if that. This means, of course, that a CD–4 recording, when taped, will lose most, if not all, of the difference signals. The 4-2-4 system can, however, be taped on a normal recorder and the play-back signals can be matrix-processed to produce a quadraphonic output.

Equipment for both the 4-2-4 and CD–4 quadraphonic systems are available in the shops and the public will eventually decide which will survive. The advantages and disadvantages of each should now be perfectly clear and can be summarized as follows:

	4-2-4	CD–4
Crosstalk between channels	Limited crosstalk is inevitable in the reproduced signals	No crosstalk other than that produced by the player cartridge
Compatability with existing stereo equipment	Compatible	Compatible, provided the player cartridge can track without appreciable distortion up to 45 kH; if not the difference signal in the groove may be damaged
Suitability for radio broadcasting	Suitable	Unsuitable, except for stereo reproduction
Suitability for tape recording	Suitable	Unsuitable except for stereo recording

Choice of Equipment

The amateur enthusiast cannot record on disc. Audio equipment for sound reproduction is, on the other hand, so easy to buy that it is equally easy to choose unwisely.

At one end of the range there are compact stereo record players available for as little as £30, even today. Yet the better off can spend as much as £200 on a good turntable, £50 on a stereo cartridge, £200 on an amplifier, and £200 for a pair of loudspeakers, making a total of £650 or more, without going in for a radio tuner or a tape deck, and without indulging in quadraphonics. So the first decision a would-be enthusiast must make is the price he is prepared to pay.

Once you are able to spend more than the price of a self-contained high-fidelity record player, you are faced with the problem of allocating your money to the various components. Should one spend more on the turntable, on the cartridge, on the amplifier or on the loudspeakers? Advice will vary but one thing is sure. An expensive amplifier and loudspeaker cannot produce high fidelity results if the cartridge output is poor. So a wise first step is to buy the best cartridge you can afford. Cartridges are not all that expensive; but the snag is that not all cartridges are compatible with every record deck and arm. So when buying a good cartridge you may also have to buy an arm recommended for use with it. If you want a semi-automatic arm (and most people do — the risk of damaging records is far less), you must take the turntable that comes with it. So your choice of cartridge will be tied up with your choice of turntable and arm.

If your cartridge is capable of delivering a high quality signal into your system, you will be unable to make the most of it unless your loudspeakers are good. So here is the second component for which it pays to buy the best you can afford.

The amplifier is a vital link between the cartridge and the loudspeakers, it is true; but amplifiers are not necessarily as good as their price. All reputable makes of amplifier are supplied with technical data which defines their frequency response and distortion levels. Where two amplifiers have equivalent specifications, the cheaper probably represents the better value for money.

In general terms a stereo high-fidelity amplifier for the home should deliver a minimum power of 4 watts per channel, and a maximum of 15 watts per channel. It is, indeed, very rare for music in the home to be played at a level which peaks in excess of 8 watts per channel, unless excessive bass is desired.

After deciding what your needs are and what your budget will allow, there will still be a variety of alternatives which may suit you. The final choice will depend partly on personal preference, and the best course is to go to a good audio store and seek demonstrations of suitable alternatives. Even better, before you make your decision, is to have a demonstration in your home. Equipment may not sound quite the same at home as it does in the studio at the store.

CHAPTER 5

Enter Magnetic Recording

Of all the popular technologies of today magnetic recording must have been by far the slowest to develop. Valdemar Poulsen, a Danish inventor from Copenhagen, built the first magnetic recorder, which he called the telegraphone, in 1898. A steel piano wire was magnetized to make the recording by passing it between the poles of a pair of electro-magnets, placed end to end and wound in series. The electronic amplifier had not yet been invented and Poulsen's recorder worked direct from a voice receiver similar to Alexander Bell's early telephone receiver, and played back direct into primitive earphones.

Poulsen's early telegraphone worked well enough to win him the Grand Prix at the Paris Exposition in 1900. It impressed businessmen and $5 million was quickly raised to form a manufacturing company in the United States. The American Telegraphone Company built and manufactured a sturdy little recorder. The machine contained a spool of wire long enough to record for 30 minutes continuously, though it travelled at 7 feet per second. But sales were disappointing. A Danish firm, formed in 1909 to build and market the telegraphone was even more unsuccessful. It collapsed after seven years without having sold a single machine.

That the telegraphone worked effectively is well documented. Oscar Dupue, in an article 'My First Fifty Years in Motion Pictures', published in the Journal of the Society of Motion Picture Engineers in December 1947, tells how he recorded Jimmie Powers on board ship in 1907 and was able to re-record the comedian's voice on film thirty years later from the original wire.

In 1912 Lee de Forest, who had by then invented the valve amplifier, experimented with the Poulsen telegraphone and foresaw a great future for the machine. Even this prediction, and the substitution of the wire by thin steel tape, did not help the American promoters to sell the machine as widely as was necessary. Eventually their company went into liquidation, as had the Danish firm.

Theory of Magnetic Recording

We have seen how sound waves are converted into electrical vibrations by means of the microphone, and how these are 'stored' on a gramophone record by reconverting them into a physical vibration which modulates the groove. A vibrating electric current can vary not only in strength but in polarity, alternating between positive and negative, and a magnetic field can also vary in strength and polarity, the latter alternating between north and south. Poulsen reasoned that if a vibrating electric current were to be passed through the windings of an electro-magnet, it would produce a vibrating magnetic field. By focusing such a field on to a steel wire, the metal would become magnetized; and by moving the wire the induced magnetism would vary along its length in step with the variations in the electric current.

(It should be noted that an electro-magnet is made of 'soft' iron, which does not retain magnetism, whereas steel, once

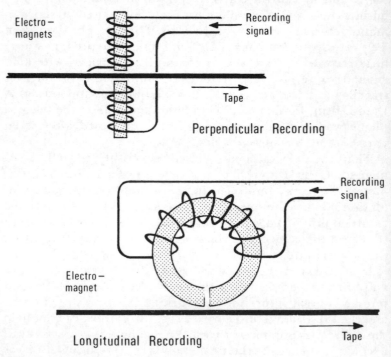

Fig. 15. The development of the record head

magnetized, retains the magnetic property, until this is altered by outside means.)

The original telegraphone recorded by passing a magnetic field right through the steel wire and the improved model, using steel tape, had a similar arrangement. Because of the physical size of the magnetic poles above and below the steel tape, this resulted in each individual magnetic impression occupying a considerable horizontal distance on the tape. This in turn meant that a relatively high tape speed was essential to avoid the waves of the higher recorded frequencies merging into each other. The substitution of the ring electro-magnetic head, which recorded from one side of the tape only, was a significant advance. The magnetic 'gap' could be less than a thousandth of an inch. This meant that the recorded wavelength on tape could be significantly shorter than before and the tape speed could be greatly reduced.

Distortion in Recording

The principal aim in all systems of recording is to produce an output signal identical with the input signal. Not only must

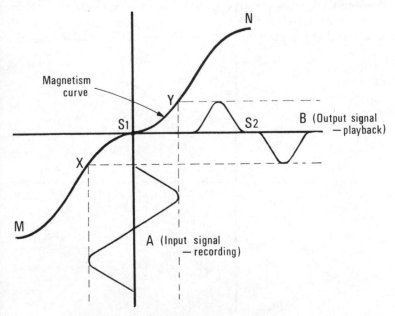

Fig. 16. Recording without bias

the frequencies of the recorded sound be faithfully reproduced, but the amplitude of each output wave must mirror
that of each input wave at any moment.

One of the problems of magnetic recording lies in the fact
that induced magnetism does not vary in direct proportion to
the current which causes it. As can be seen in Fig. 16, there is a
'step' in the magnetism curve (MN) at the point where polarity
changes from north to south. This results in a distorted recording. If you take a recording signal (A), consisting of a sine
wave, the step (S1) in the induced magnetism at the polarity
change produces a corresponding step (S2) at the point of
change from positive to negative in the recorded signal (B).
This results in a distorted sound on playback. In order to avoid
the step in the magnetism curve Poulsen added a fixed voltage
(bias) to the input signal so that the alternating voltage never
crossed the zero point.

The output (B) on playback was now an alternating current
which, resulting from a relatively straight portion of the
magnetism curve (XY), avoided the step and followed the
input signal (A) fairly accurately. The disadvantage of
Poulsen's DC (direct current) bias system was that only a relatively short portion (XY) of the magnetism curve was used.
The resulting signal was therefore weak in relation to the

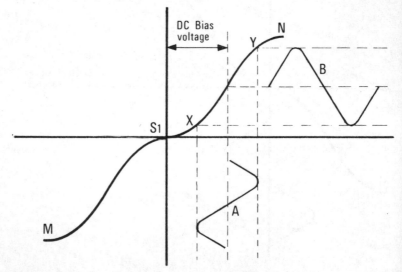

Fig. 17. Recording with DC bias

natural hiss always caused by unmagnetized tape passing the playback head. The signal-to-noise ratio was poor.

AC Bias Introduced

DC bias was used in all the early recorders and it was not until W. L. Carlson and G. W. Carpenter of the United States Naval Research Laboratory devised the modern system of AC bias that tape output and the signal-to-noise ratio could be significantly improved. In their system, instead of adding a fixed bias voltage to the input signal, they added an alternating voltage. The frequency of this voltage was well above the top limit of hearing so that, if reproduced, it would not be heard.

The input signal (A), consisting of the AC bias added to the audio signal, now had the waveform shown in the accompanying Fig. 18, and the output signal (B) had the waveform seen on the right. The output voltage has a step in each wave (E), as it crosses from positive to negative polarity, but its modulation 'envelope' remains undistorted. In fact there are now two undistorted audio signals (C and D), which can be combined

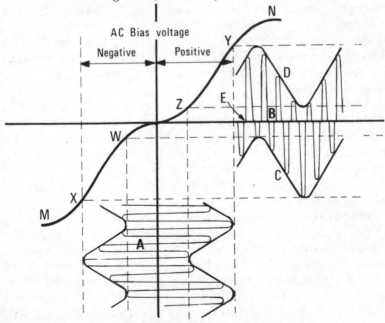

Fig. 18. Recording with AC bias

electronically to produce a single powerful output. Not only does this result in a greatly improved signal-to-noise ratio, but it was found that the natural tape 'hiss' was itself significantly less when recording with AC bias.

Tape Erasure

In order to erase a signal from a tape, the minute magnetic particles in the coating must all have their individual magnetic fields either cancelled, or else uniformly orientated so that no audible signal will be produced when the tape is passed over a playback head. In the early days the method of erasure was to pass the tape through a powerful fixed magnetic field so that the magnetic particles would all be left with their own tiny fields equal in strength and with their magnetic axes parallel.

This certainly erased the signal, but as the actual magnetic particles are neither uniform in size nor arranged with their physical axes parallel, tapes erased by this method produced considerable background hiss on playback.

When the AC bias method was invented it was discovered that an alternating AC field, provided the frequency was high enough, produced efficient erasure with considerably less residual background noise.

As AC bias required an AC oscillator to produce the bias current, it was common sense to use the same oscillator output to power an electro-magnetic erase head, and this is what is done to this day.

It was found in practice that in order to avoid high pitched whistles (heterodynes) the bias frequency used must be at least four and preferably five times the highest recorded audio frequency. This meant that on a high-fidelity recording systems, designed to record and reproduce sounds up to 15 kHz, the bias frequency needed to be not less than 60 kHz and preferably 75 kHz.

In the case of the erase current considerable power is needed to ensure full erasure, and the higher the frequency the more difficult it is to produce power. So while the bias frequency could, in theory, be much higher than the minimum of 60 kHz, it was cheaper, when it came to erasure, to keep the frequency down to this minimum. Today 60 kHz is a commonly used standard, though inexpensive machines recording only up to 8 or 9 kHz use a lower bias frequency (sometimes as low as 35 kHz) and in more expensive equipment the frequency is raised to 80 kHz or more.

Tape Transport

There are two kinds of distortion possible in tape recording and reproduction. Once the problem of electronic distortion has been solved there remains the possibility of mechanical distortion caused by tiny variations in tape speed.

We all know what happens when the speed of rotation of a gramophone record is uneven. The same trouble arises when the speed of travel of magnetic tape across either the record head or the playback head is not constant.

The terms used for this type of 'speed' distortion are 'wow' and 'flutter'. Both terms refer, in fact, to the same fault; a variation in the pitch of reproduced sound due to irregular tape speed. The difference is in the frequency of the irregularity. Wow is a slow variation, easily heard on long sustained musical notes. It sounds like a slow vibrato with a frequency of anything between one second and about a fifth of a second. Flutter is the result of more rapid speed variations up to a frequency of about 25 Hz.

To ensure a constant tape speed the modern tape recorder has what is known as capstan drive. The capstan is an accurately machined rotating steel shaft which is powered by a constant speed electric motor and fixed to a heavy flywheel

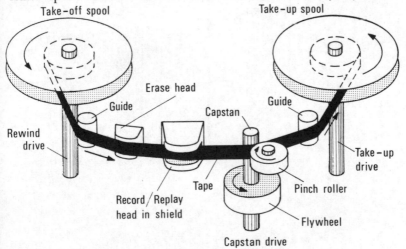

Fig. 19. Standard reel-to-reel tape system

designed to provide added stability in the speed of rotation. The tape is passed between the capstan and a composition pinch-roller which presses the tape tightly against the capstan in order to ensure a firm friction grip.

Fig. 19 shows a typical tape transport system.

The Induction Motor

While a heavy flywheel will tend to 'iron out' variations in capstan speed, the drive motor must itself be designed to provide constant power at constant speed. The induction motor, which uses the frequency of alternating current to govern its speed, is the answer.

While the design of induction motors varies in detail, the principle is simple. If you suspend a small bar magnet between the poles of a large horseshoe magnet, the bar will rotate until the opposing poles, which attract one another, are nearest. If you could now change the polarity of the fixed magnet, north becoming south and vice versa, the small magnet, free to rotate in a horizontal plane, would immediately swing round, so that its north pole would again be as near as possible to the fixed magnet's south pole, and its south pole nearest to the other's north. If the fixed magnet is replaced by an electromagnet, the windings of which are fed with an alternating

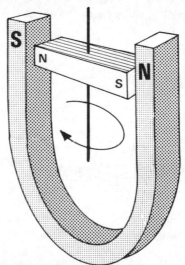

Fig. 20. Principle of induction motor

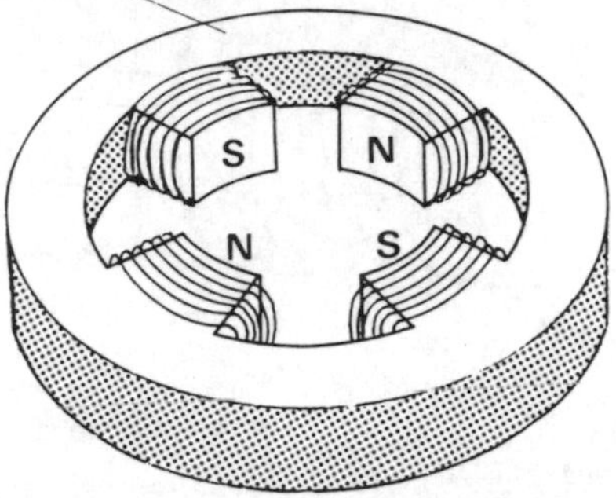

Soft iron core made up
of many thin laminations

Fig. 21. Lay-out of 4-pole induction motor stator

current, its poles will change place twice for each complete AC cycle. Using the 50 Hz mains in the United Kingdom, there will be 100 polarity changes a second. In order to follow these polarity changes the suspended magnet would have to turn 50 revolutions each second.

The modern induction motor has a large electro-magnetic 'stator', the coils of which are fed with alternating current. While a two-pole stator is sometimes used, a four-pole, six-pole, or even an eight-pole stator is more common. Obviously the greater the number of poles the shorter the distance through which the 'suspended' magnet must rotate for it to achieve equilibrium.

The rotor of the induction motor is not, in fact, a suspended magnet. Instead it is built up of a stack of iron laminations with a series of insulated copper conductors running longitudinally in grooves, these being connected to shorting rings at each end. When suspended on its rotating shaft, within the pole pieces of the stator, the alternating magnetic field from the stator poles induces currents in the conductors of the rotor. These currents produce a system of magnetic fields which 'replace' those of our imaginary suspended magnet. They react with the fields of the stator and attempt to turn the rotor to the position where unlike fields will be closest and like fields most distant. As the stator field alternates, the rotor continues to rotate (Fig. 22).

If the rotor were to rotate at exactly the speed at which the stator field alternates, the magnetic lines of force would no

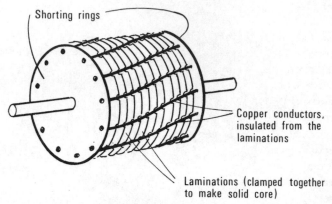

Shorting rings

Copper conductors, insulated from the laminations

Laminations (clamped together to make solid core)

Fig. 22. Construction of induction motor rotor

longer move in relation to the rotor conductors, and the rotor conductors would no longer produce magnetic fields. There would then be no force to keep the rotor turning and it would begin to slow down. The more the rotor speed lags behind the alternating field of the stator, the greater the speed with which the lines of magnetic force cross the conductors and the greater the induced magnetic field.

As the latter grows the rotor tends to move faster, so reducing the difference between the speed of change of the stator's electro-magnetic field and the rotor's rotation. In practice equilibrium is set up with the rotor speed lagging a fixed amount behind the speed of change of the stator field. The difference between the two speeds depends on the external load on the rotor, and as long as this remains unchanged its speed also remains constant.

The Synchronous Motor

The induction motor is commonly used in portable tape recorders. It is reliable and rugged and has only one disadvantage. As the rotor speed depends on the load, as well as on the frequency of the current, fluctuations in voltage affect its speed of rotation. For this reason professional tape recorders are fitted with more expensive synchronous motors of more advanced design. Though based on the induction motor principle, these motors are designed so that the rotor turns at a speed which 'locks' on to the alternating current frequency. Its speed thus depends only on the frequency and not on the load or voltage.

Direct Current Motors

Battery recorders cannot have AC motors and the speed of rotation of a simple DC motor is subject to considerable variation due to the voltage drop which occurs when a dry cell is providing power. To achieve constant speed, battery recorders normally have an electric governor which consists, basically, of a centrifugal switch which cuts out when the motor speed exceeds a preset value. Sufficiently sensitive switches can be designed to ensure a relatively constant drive speed and as the contacts of such switches tend to deteriorate when handling power, resulting in sparking which causes electrical noise in the recording system, these switches are not always used to control the motor directly. Instead they are often used to control the bias of a transistor which in turn controls the motor current.

Mechanical Linkage

The tape recorder motor has three functions. The first is to drive the capstan. It has also to keep the tape take-up spool turning and to provide power for fast rewind and wind-on.

While various systems are used, a common arrangement for capstan drive is to allow an idler wheel with a composition 'tyre' to engage the motor shaft on the one hand, and a machined circumference of the capstan flywheel on the other.

On single motor recorders the take-up spool is usually turned by means of a belt and pulley system which has sufficient slip to allow for the difference in speed between a nearly

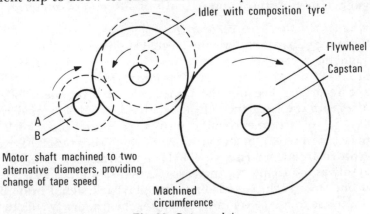

Fig. 23. Capstan drive

empty take-up spool and a nearly full one, which obviously rotates much slower. Belt drive is also used on single motor
machines for fast wind-on and rewind.

While many tape recorders derive all the drive functions
from a single induction motor, the more expensive models
have three. One of these operates the capstan only; a second is
used for take-up and fast wind-on; the third is used for the
rewind function.

Tape Speed

We have already seen that the ability of a tape recorder to
record, and playback high frequencies, depends on the size of
the magnetic gap of the record/playback head, and also on
the tape speed.

Modern head gaps are such that a relatively level frequency
response can be achieved from 30 Hz up to 16 Hz or more at a
tape speed of 19 cm/sec ($7\frac{1}{2}$ inches per second), from 40 Hz to
12.5 kHz at 9.5 cm/sec ($3\frac{3}{4}$ inches per second) and from 45 Hz
to 6.5 kHz at 4.8 cm/sec ($1\frac{7}{8}$ inches per second). As the second
of these specifications is more than adequate for the average
listener, many of the less expensive reel-to-reel tape recorders
operate at a tape speed of 9.5 cm/sec. More expensive models
have a dual or even a triple speed facility, and this is usually
achieved by having parts of the drive motor shaft machined to
different diameters. The idler wheel between the motor and
the flywheel is designed to engage the different diameter sections of the motor shaft at the turn of a knob. An alternative
system is to substitute capstan shafts of different diameters.

Equalization in Tape-Recording

We saw in Chapter 3 how the electrical signal generated by a
magnetic record player cartridge has to be doctored, or
'equalized' to produce a level response. The same is true in
tape recording because the impedance of a magnetic head
varies with the frequency of the recorded sound. Unequalized
playback of a tape-recording results, at a tape speed of 9.5
cm/sec ($3\frac{3}{4}$ in/sec), in an output level which rises rapidly as the
recorded frequency rises to 4 kHz, and then falls even more
rapidly as the frequency increases further. To produce a level
output from such a recording, the playback signal must be
adapted so that its level falls steadily as the frequency rises to 4
kHz, and then rises again for higher frequencies. The record-

ing characteristic, when using a tape speed of 19 cm/sec (7½ in/sec) is of similar shape, but the output peak in this case is at 8 kHz.

Because the magnetic recording characteristic varies with tape speed, tape-recorders which can record at more than one speed have alternative equalization circuits which are switched in and out as the speed is changed.

Modern Recording Tape

The steel wire, and later the thin steel tape, used on the earliest magnetic recorders, was relatively heavy, and difficult to handle and to store. The idea of coating a thin non-metallic tape with a magnetizable substance had occurred to several experimenters in the late 1920s but it was Fritz Pfleumer, an engineer of Dresden, who secured a patent in February 1929 for coating a tape of paper or acetate film with a substance containing 'a powder of soft iron'. He was so far ahead of his time that he even proposed, in his patent, adding a magnetic stripe to cinema films for the making of sound movies. As Pfleumer was, apparently, unable to raise capital to produce magnetic tape himself, he persuaded AEG of Berlin to take up his invention. At first AEG ran into difficulties, but by August 1935 they had produced both a successful tape-recorder, the Magnetophone, and successful recording tape based on cellulose acetate coated with carbonyl iron powder. Before long the tape coating of iron particles began to give way to iron oxide preparations which gave improved performance, and in January 1938 the performance of the Magnetophone, using improved tapes, was considered good enough for its adoption by the German radio authorities for broadcast service.

Paper tapes continued to be used by the Germans during the war and around the world until 1947. Up to that date experiments using a plastic-based tape had been unsuccessful as no one had been able to produce a tape which combined sufficient strength without a tendency to stretch. It was then, in 1947, that the 3M company of America introduced the first successful plastic-based recording tape, with a new red oxide coating which gave considerably improved high frequency response, due to its particles being needle-shaped instead of spherical. This was the first of a new generation of recording tape which had come to stay.

In recent years there have been several advances in tape technology. The well-established ferric oxide coating can now be modified with the addition of cobalt so that it retains a greater magnetic energy, resulting in a playback output on standard equipment about 3 dB higher than was previously considered normal. And an entirely new coating, based on chromium dioxide, holds even greater magnetic energy, giving a playback output as much as 6 dB higher than standard ferric oxide tape. Unfortunately chromium dioxide requires specially designed high energy record/replay and erase heads, as well as different equalization. It can therefore only be used on recorders designed specially for it.

Advantages of Tape Recording
Tape recording has three great advantages.

In the first place playback is immediate as no processing is involved.

The second major advantage is that tape can easily be edited, by cutting and joining. While it would be a tedious task, it is even possible, for example, to cut out the clicks from a recording of a scratched gramophone record.

The third advantage of tape is the ease with which stereo recordings can be made. All that is needed is a double head which records two parallel tracks on the tape. A similar double playback head (which may be the same as the recording head) 'reads' the two parallel signals simultaneously, feeding the resulting signals to two separate amplifiers and so to a pair of loudspeakers. Quadraphonic recording and playback is similarly easy.

If tape recording has advantages, it has disadvantages too. Tape is thin and can be more easily damaged than a disc. The electrical noise arising from magnetic tape is generally greater than that produced by a clean vinyl disc, though we shall see in the next chapter how electronic means of suppressing tape 'hiss' have been developed. Thirdly, tape recording copies cannot be mass produced as discs are. A 30-minute long playing record is stamped in a matter of seconds; but to copy a tape, the master tape — and the tapes on which the sound is to be copied — must be run through an electronic reproducer from start to finish.

Tape Jointing

It is not difficult for the amateur to make highly 'professional' joins in tape; but some 'know-how' is required. The system, basically, is that of butt jointing, using special fine adhesive tape over the back of the join. When joining most recordings it is generally best to make the butt joint diagonally, as this results in a very even transition of sound across the join. The simplest method of cutting is to overlap the two tapes to be joined and to cut neatly across both simultaneously with scissors. Next lay a short length of adhesive jointing tape, sticky side up, on a flat surface. (You should use the special jointing tape made for this purpose, as ordinary transparent office tape is thicker and deteriorates with age). Next place the tapes to be joined, with the cut ends touching but not overlapping, on the sticky tape. Finally trim off the excess jointing tape. Make sure that your tape-cutting scissors have not acquired any magnetism; otherwise the join will probably produce a click when the tape is played back.

When editing speech the tape is best cut straight across at right angles. This is because cuts must be made between words, and the gap may be too short for a diagonal cut. To locate the exact spot for such a cut, the recorder should be switched for playback with the tape removed from between the capstan and the pinch roller. The tape is then slid slowly across the playback head by hand while listening carefully.

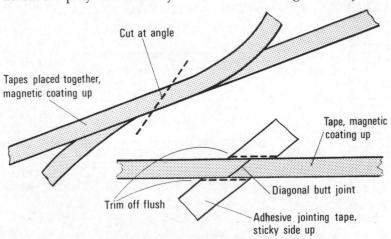

Fig. 24. Method of tape jointing

Tape and Track Dimensions

Standard tape used on reel-to-reel recorders is 6.35mm ($\frac{1}{4}$ in.) wide. Professional machines sometimes use the entire tape width for a mono recording, but domestic mono recorders more usually record on half the tape width. The tape can then be used for separate recordings in each direction, thus doubling the total playing time. In theory a full track recording should give twice the output from the playback head, which means a better signal-to-noise ratio, as electrical noise originating in the amplifier will be the same in either case. In practice, however, a half-track recording produces more than half the useful output of a full-track recording.

For twin track mono recording the two tracks are each 2.5mm wide, with an unused 1.35mm gap between. The gap ensures no crosstalk.

In the case of stereo recordings the professional machine uses two tracks recorded simultaneously side by side, with stacked record and playback heads. The track dimensions and gap are the same as for twin-track mono recording.

Most domestic stereo reel-to-reel tape recorders employ a four-track system, using alternate tracks for each stereo pair.

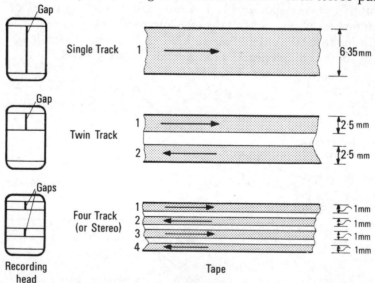

Fig. 25. Single, twin-track and four-track tapes, with corresponding gaps on the recording heads

In this case the tracks are each 1mm wide, the three gaps between the four tracks being each 0.78mm in width.

Modern recording tape is manufactured in a variety of thicknesses, the thickness determining the length of tape on the spool and the resulting playing time. Standard play tape of 360m (1,200 ft) length, which is strong and easy to handle and to edit, is accommodated on an 18cm (7in.) spool. This provides approximately 64 minutes of play, at 9.5cm/sec ($3\frac{3}{4}$ in./sec) in each direction. A 13cm (5in.) spool holds 180m (600 ft) of this tape.

Long-play, double- and triple-play tape, as their names suggest, provide extended, two and three times the playing time on the same sized spool. Long-play tape is excellent for four-track recorders and can be edited with care. Double- and triple-play tape is not easy to edit, and the latter is so delicate that it is easily damaged. Also they should not be heavily modulated, as there is a risk in such cases of 'print-through'. This means that, over a period of time, the sound recorded on one portion of tape partially magnetizes the coatings of the turns of tape lying adjacent to it on the reel, producing a distant repeat on playback.

Head Magnetism

After long use the record/playback head of a recorder inevitably acquires some residual magnetism, especially where recording has been at a high signal level. Such residual magnetism results in excessive tape noise and to avoid this tape-recorder heads should be periodically demagnetized. Once a year is appropriate in most cases, though where a recorder is in constant use this may become necessary more often. A head demagnetizer is a simple gadget which produces a powerful alternating magnetic field at the end of its probe. To use it the probe is first placed against the front surface of the record/playback head. The current is then switched on. Finally the probe is withdrawn gradually from the head, and the current is only switched off when it has been completely withdrawn.

The Tape-recorder's Versatility

Today the tape-recorder is very widely used, and is the basis of all modern professional recording. When a band or orchestra

is recorded the sound of different parts of the ensemble is partially isolated and recorded separately on several tracks on a
single standard tape. The recording engineer can then alter
the gain and even the tone of each track independently on
playback, to produce the most acceptable mixture of sound
when making a master disc, for example. When an orchestra
plays a long work there may be flaws in the performance. If
the work is recorded a second time these flaws may be avoided,
while others may occur. An expert sound engineer can edit the
tapes, replacing the flaws on one performance with improved
passages from the other, and this can be done so that the
listener will never know that the final version is blended from
two or more performances. The result, amazingly, is that
modern recordings offer 'performances' which may be better
than is humanly possible in any single live exposition.

The tape-recorder can be conveniently used by the amateur
photographer to provide a commentary mixed with sound
effects and background music for a slide show. A spare track
on the tape can also be used to provide electric pulses which
operate the projector, thus changing the slides automatically
at the right moment. Philips produce a handy pulse synchronizer for this purpose. It stands close to the tape-recorder and
the tape is routed around the synchronizer's head either before
it enters the tape deck assembly, or after it emerges from it.
This gadget makes and reads pulses on the lowest quarter of
the tape, leaving the top three quarters free. The synchronizer
can thus be used either with a two-track mono recorder, which
modulates the top half of the tape, or with a 4-track stereo
recorder using tracks 1 and 3 for sound.

Miniaturized battery recorders, too, have many uses. They
can be set up for interviews or conferences, or taken into the
country to record birdsong or rural sound effects for amateur
dramatics.

CHAPTER 6

Hi-Fi on Tape

The performance of modern record/playback heads, and of modern tape, is so good that tape-recordings can be made to reproduce sound with absolute fidelity, provided the limitations of the tape-recorder are known and allowed for.

Cleaning and Oiling

We have already seen that the recorder must have a well-designed tape transport system if wow and flutter are to be avoided. Another essential is cleanliness. The tape guides must be kept clean so that friction is minimal. The motor, idler and capstan bearings must be kept lightly oiled. Above all, the surface of the pinch roller must be kept clean and dry.

After oiling the bearings, which should be done about twice a year if the recorder is well used, all excess oil must be removed. If oil creeps up to the tape you will be in trouble.

The simplest way of cleaning the tape guides is to use methylated spirit and a fine dry cloth. One manufacturer recommends the use of 'cotton buds', tiny wads of cotton wool fixed to the ends of light plastic sticks and sold by chemists for cleaning babies' noses and ears. These can be helpful provided you make sure no loose cotton gets caught on projections.

Spirit and cotton buds are also fine for cleaning record/replay and erase heads. Frequent use of a recorder results inevitably in a minute deposit of the tape's magnetic coating building up. Any such deposit on the heads will reduce the intimacy of contact between the tape coating and the magnetic gap and this will impair the frequency response. You cannot overdo head cleaning, provided you do not rub too hard. Once each time the recorder is used is not overdoing it.

The Problem of Tape Noise

Tape noise (a soft 'hiss') is inherent in tape recordings and can become a nuisance. On the other hand it can be sufficiently minimized for sound reproduced from tape to qualify fully for the term 'high fidelity'. A number of factors are involved.

The first and most important is the use of good quality tape.

Tape noise depends partly on the nature of the tape coating and modern low-noise high-output tapes offer the highest signal-to-noise ratio. So these should be used.

It was explained in the previous chapter how magnetic heads in continual use tend to acquire some residual magnetism. It was also explained how this is removed by the use of a specially made de-magnetizing instrument. Periodic demagnetization of the heads is essential if tape noise is to be kept to a minimum. It is possible for little or no residual magnetism to be acquired by the heads over a year or more of use, if the recording level is kept relatively low (this will be explained later in this chapter), but demagnetization once a month would not be out of place as a routine measure for any well-used recorder. Other steel components, such as guides, with which the tape coating comes in contact should also be demagnetized.

The perception of tape hiss is dependent on the loudness of the recorded sound. During silent passages between the sentences of a recorded conversation, or immediately before or after a passage of music, the tape hiss can be clearly heard. Immediately the recorded sound is loud enough the difference in level between the hiss and the sound ensures that only the wanted sound can be heard. During soft music both the noise and the music may be heard together.

The Theory of Noise Suppression
This question of the relative loudness of tape noise and recorded sound gives the clue to the possibility of noise suppression by electronic means. If soft sounds could be sufficiently amplified before recording to give them a dynamic level sufficiently above that of the playback tape hiss, it would then be possible to reproduce with the playback amplifier at a low enough level for the tape hiss to be inaudible. Then the only extraneous noise in soft passages would be that generated in the amplifier itself — not a serious problem. This theory is fine. But if this is done for soft passages, trouble arises when loud music is recorded. The basic problem lies in the fact that recorded tape has a limited dynamic range.

The lower limit of a tape-recorder's dynamic range is set by the tape noise. Most of the better tape decks have meters which indicate the upper limit of loudness that can be recorded with-

out distortion. At this point in loudness the tape coating is
saturated with magnetism. This means that it cannot be magnetized much more, certainly not without a distorted result.
This, then, marks the upper limit of loudness which can be
properly recorded. The lower and upper limits define the
dynamic range of the tape, and usually this is around 60 dB,
sometimes a little more.

The orchestra, on the other hand, regularly uses a dynamic
range between the softest and loudest passages of 90 dB and
sometimes even as much as 100 dB. This means that if a soft
passage of music is recorded at a sufficiently high level for the
tape noise not to intrude, loud passages will inevitably be distorted, unless the gain control is turned down in the meanwhile. On the other hand, if the gain control is first adjusted so
that the loudest sounds to be recorded do not exceed the
saturation point of the tape, as indicated by the meter, subse-
quent soft passages will be recorded at so low a level that tape
noise will certainly mar the sound on playback.

If a recordist were to turn the gain control up when soft
passages are being recorded, and down for loud passages, the
recording would have a compressed version of the original
sound so far as loudness was concerned. When played back
there would be no audible hiss over soft notes, and no distortion on loud, and it would, in theory, be possible to restore the
original dynamic range during playback by turning the gain
control down for the soft passages, and up for the loud. In
other words the gain would be manipulated in exactly the
opposite manner to that used for recording.

Electronics is so versatile that one would imagine that a
clever engineer could design circuits which would automatically carry out the processes of dynamic compression
during recording and expansion during playback. Indeed
many electronic engineers have devised such circuits. Unfortunately few of them approach perfection in their action,
the problem lying in the fact that a circuit cannot anticipate a
change of loudness; it can only operate as a result of that
change.

Another problem lies in the fact that it is perfectly possible
in music to have (to suggest an extreme example), a loud high-
pitched trumpet playing to a soft bass background. How will
an electronic circuit know whether to raise the gain, so that

the soft bass is kept above the tape hiss level, or reduce it so that the trumpet's sound does not over-modulate the tape and become distorted?

The Dolby System
While a number of manufacturers have managed to produce reasonably efficient circuits, these all have weaknesses. It was not until an American named Dolby sought a new approach, that a system which really works effectively was designed. In the simplest terms (the system is, in practice, complex and consequently expensive), the Dolby system divides the signal into different frequency bands, dynamic compression and expansion being carried out independently within each band.

For the amateur the Dolby B system, which is somewhat simpler and cheaper than the Dolby A system used on professional machines, is economic and well worth the expense. It results in considerably increased clarity in a tape recording, significantly reduces the effects of hum and rumble in the low frequencies, and of hiss in the high frequencies. So popular is Dolby B circuitry becoming among audiophiles that musical recordings in cassette form are available recorded with Dolby B compression, so that they can immediately be played back on equipment which incorporates the Dolby B circuit.

The Cassette and the Cartridge
So far we have spoken mainly of reel-to-reel recorders using $\frac{1}{4}$in. tape which is run, as a rule, either at 19cm (7$\frac{1}{2}$in.), or at 9.5cm (3$\frac{3}{4}$in.) per second.

As long as it is used intelligently, open reel tape has a great deal to offer as a recording medium. It is, however, delicate and must be handled with patience and care. For the impatient man or woman who is not interested in editing, there was obviously a need for a simplified method of putting tape on the recorder, a method which would protect the delicate medium from the dangers of careless handling. Two solutions were evolved — the cassette and the cartridge.

The Tape Cassette
Originated by the Dutch company, Philips, a decision was taken early to design a system which would not only keep tape protected and make threading a simple process, but would

make possible the design and manufacture of really small portable tape-recorders. Advantage was taken of the improvements in head design and tape coatings which had resulted in increased output and improved frequency response. Because of the latter it was decided to adopt 4.75cm ($1\frac{7}{8}$in.) per second as the operating tape speed, and because of the increased output it was considered feasible to reduce the width of the tape to 3.8mm ($\frac{5}{32}$in.). The resulting 'compact' cassette, as it was originally called, was indeed extremely compact, and because the tape remains entirely within the perimeter of the thin plastic container, it was also decided that thin double- and triple-play tape could be safely used.

The cassette has become so popular that it hardly needs description. Figure 26 shows the internal layout. It fits into the recorder so that the feed and take-up spool hubs locate on two protruding shafts, which provide rotation for take-up, wind-on and rewind. At the same time a tiny protruding steel capstan fits through the right hand hole near the front edge of the cassette, passing behind the tape. When the cassette recorder is set in the operating mode, the erase head and the record/replay head move into the left hand and middle gaps in the edge of the cassette, pressing against the tape. Behind the middle gap is a tiny spring-mounted felt pressure pad which keeps the tape in close contact with the record/replay

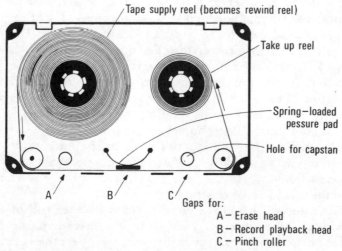

Fig. 26. Internal layout of tape cassette

head. Along with the two heads, a pinch roller moves forward into the right hand gap in the cassette edge, pushing the tape against the capstan. Unlike in the reel-to-reel recorder the tape in a cassette is wound so that its coating faces outward.

The C60 cassette holds 92m (300ft) of long-play tape, giving a playing time of 30 minutes in one direction. As in the reel-to-reel recorder, two tracks are used for mono and four for stereo recording, the tracks being scaled down from those used on standard tape. As the cassette is symmetrical it can be used either side up, providing twice the playing time of a single run through. The same applies to C90 cassettes (45 minutes in each direction) and C120 (60 minutes in each direction).

In the case of stereo recording on cassette, instead of using tracks 1 and 3 for the stereo pair, as in standard tape recorders, the cassette recorder uses the top two adjacent quarter tracks, the lower two coming into play when the cassette is turned over. This enables a cassette recorded in stereo to be played back on a mono recorder, and vice versa.

The Cartridge
The American designed cartridge is a continuous play device which accommodates a single reel of standard $\frac{1}{4}$in. tape used at 9.5cm ($3\frac{3}{4}$in.) per second. The tape is wound loosely around a fixed hub — so loosely that it can be pulled out from the centre of the reel, feeding askew, so that it passes across the wound tape via guides which feed it along one edge of the cartridge, behind gaps similar to those in the cassette. The cartridge contains its own pinch roller against which the tape is pressed by the capstan as the cartridge is pushed into the recorder. As the tape is transported past the replay head by the action of the capstan and pinch roller, it continues feeding from the centre of the roll, rotating the roll as it does so. The tape is continuous, one end being joined to the other permanently, so that the rotating roll pulls in the loose tape end, providing its own take-up. There is therefore no need for powered take-up. As the tape is continuous there is also no need for a wind-on or rewind facility.

The standard cartridge holds a 3in. diameter coil of tape providing 20 minutes of playing time. Instead of the four tracks normally used on the reel-to-reel recorder, the cartridge player accommodates eight, arranged in four stereo pairs. A

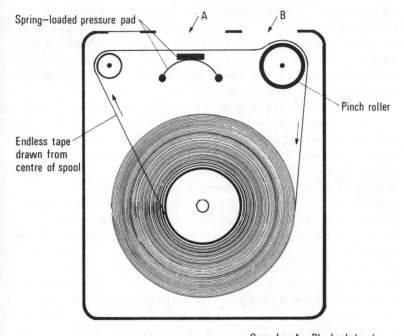

Spring—loaded pressure pad

A

B

Pinch roller

Endless tape
drawn from
centre of spool

Gaps for: A— Playback head
B— Capstan

Fig. 27. Internal layout of 8-track cartridge

recorded programme in stereo thus lasts for 80 minutes.

The stereo pairs are located well apart. Tracks 1 and 5 form a pair, tracks 2 and 6 making up the next; and so on.

The endless loop of tape includes a metal foil strip which operates a solenoid which in turn moves the replay head down one track each time it comes round. In this way playback is continuous.

The cartridge is used mainly only for prerecorded programmes, and is particularly useful for installation in cars. It has the disadvantage that it must be played from the point at which playback was last stopped. Due to its faster tape speed it should provide a somewhat better acoustic performance than the cassette. There is no provision for erasure.

The Microphone in Tape Recording

There is a vital difference between a microphone and the human ear which must be appreciated if the former is to be used to best advantage. This difference lies in the fact that human ears normally work in pairs linked by the brain. There are tiny phase and level differences between the response of each ear to a particular sound. The brain 'reads' these differences and can determine, with a fair degree of accuracy, the direction from which the sound came and, to some extent, the distance of its source.

This human ability to locate a sound is particularly important when listening in a confined space because, unless the wall, floor and ceiling are all covered with sound-absorbent material, sounds will be reflected and the ear will hear the reflections as well as the original sounds. Fortunately these reflections come from different directions, and the two ears (backed by the brain's ability to interpret the two sets of information) make it possible for one to 'listen' to the original sound, the reflections being mentally relegated to giving an impression of the general environment.

The information from the ear is also coordinated, if the source of the sound is visible, with the information sent to the brain by the eyes. The result is that the human being can not only 'locate' a sound, but can 'discriminate' between sounds. This means, for example, that if you or I were listening to people talking in a crowded room, we could concentrate our attention on the voice of a single person and listen to what he is saying while keeping the other voices, as well as the confusing sound reflections from walls and elsewhere, in a mental background.

When a single microphone picks up sound and this is reproduced on a loudspeaker, a listener receives the information second hand. His ears give him information on the location and distance of the loudspeaker, and not of the original sound. If the loudspeaker is visible, the eye will do the same.

A normal omni-directional microphone can also not discriminate between an original sound and its reflections from walls or other surfaces. The result is that when its signal is heard through a loudspeaker the listener hears the sound and its reflections all coming from the same direction. No longer is the listener's brain able to discriminate between the two and the resulting combination reduces clarity.

Microphone design can help here. Not all microphones are omni-directional, and a design which accepts more sound from the front than from the back and sides will add clarity by reducing some of the reflected sound. With this type of microphone the signal contains a greater proportion of the original sound and less of the reflected sound.

When reproduced the listener hears this improved signal from the loudspeaker, along with reflection from the listening room walls. As the ears can discriminate against the latter, clarity is largely preserved.

When two microphones are used as a stereo pair the aim is to give the ears of each listener a pair of signals with phase and level differences similar to those which a listener would have heard if he had been listening to the original sounds. When earphones are used and the eyes are kept shut the result can be a highly realistic stereo image. Using loudspeakers, the objective is more difficult to achieve as the stereo image will depend partly on where the listener and his ears are located in relation to the loudspeakers; listening room sound reflections will also be added. Nor can the listener's eyes give added information on the source of the perceived sounds. All they can see are the loudspeakers

We can see now that there is a great deal of difference between the use of the single microphone and the use of a stereo pair; in practice, it is often easier to produce an acceptable result when recording live in stereo than it is in mono.

Having understood the problems involved we are now ready to learn how best to use the microphone. Before we do so, however, we need to know of the different kinds of microphone.

Microphone Types

The microphone is designed to do what the loudspeaker does in reverse. It converts the alternating pressure waves of sound into corresponding alternating electrical waves. A moving coil loudspeaker will work as a microphone. The same unit is often used for both functions in the office intercom and in office dictating machines which allow one to play back through the recording 'microphone'.

However, the dynamic microphone, as this moving coil type is called, is only one of five main types. The others are the carbon microphone, the crystal microphone, the condenser microphone and the ribbon microphone.

The Carbon Microphone

The carbon microphone was used in the early days of radio but today it is confined almost entirely to the telephone. This is because its output varies with frequency and its signal-to-noise ratio is low. The telephone does not require high fidelity reproduction and it so happens that the output characteristic of the carbon microphone is such that it converts that part of the sound spectrum most needed for speech clarity in a relatively noisy background. Simple and cheap to manufacture, the carbon microphone consists of a metal diaphragm behind which is a layer of loosely packed carbon granules. It operates as an electrical resistance which varies according to the pressure on the diaphragm. It must therefore be used with a low-voltage battery; an electric current passes continually through the instrument, this current varying as an analogue of the sound waves which cause the diaphragm to vibrate.

The Crystal Microphone

The crystal microphone uses the same principle as the crystal gramophone pick-up to convert physical movement into an electric signal. A vibrating diaphragm is fixed so that it exerts a vibrating pressure on a thin slice of Rochelle salt or similar piezoelectric crystal. The vibrating pressure produced in the crystal induces a vibrating electrical voltage across it. The crystal microphone can be designed to produce a relatively level response over the audio spectrum and it is not unduly costly.

The Condenser Microphone

As its name implies this microphone is constructed as a capacitor; the metal diaphragm is separated from a metal back plate by a tiny air gap, usually around 0.025mm (about a thousandth of an inch). When the diaphragm vibrates the capacitance varies, and by including it in a suitable circuit an electrical analogue of the original sound waves can be secured. Condenser microphones generally provide a very level frequency response and are suitable for high-fidelity work. They are very sensitive but they need a voltage to enable them to work. Nowadays it is common practice to build a tiny transistor amplifier into the microphone housing, power being obtained from a dry cell.

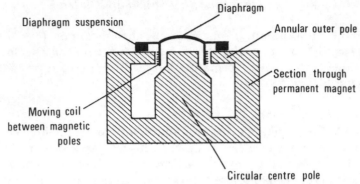

Fig. 28 Components of dynamic microphone

The Dynamic Microphone

The dynamic microphone, as already explained, is similar in principle to the moving coil loudspeaker. Instead of a large cone to propagate sound, the diaphragm of this microphone is usually no larger than the voice coil. This is a widely used microphone which gives a wide and fairly level frequency response. It is very robust.

The Ribbon Microphone

This microphone is excellent for recording high-quality sound, especially complicated sound such as that produced by an orchestra. It is delicate, however, and must be treated with care. The diaphragm consists of a thin almost weightless

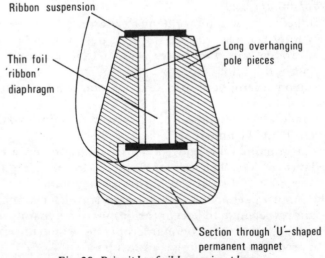

Fig. 29. Principle of ribbon microphone

ribbon of aluminium, usually about 0.0025mm (one ten thousandth of an inch) thick, suspended between the long parallel poles of a specially designed permanent magnet assembly (Fig. 29).

Breast Microphone
On TV one sometimes sees a small microphone hung on a cord around a man's neck, or clipped to his tie like a tie-pin. It is important to realize that a standard microphone will not give a satisfactory response used in this way as the higher frequencies of the voice are directed forward in a narrow angle from the mouth, whereas the lower frequencies radiate in all directions. The breast or 'Lavalier' microphone is designed with a reduced bass and an exaggerated high frequency response so that the loss of voice quality due to the microphone's position will be automatically compensated.

Radio Microphone
This is a microphone with a miniature battery-powered radio transmitter built into its case. The radio signal is picked up by a receiver up to 15 or 20 metres away and then passed to the associated amplifier. In this way there need be no cable from the microphone to the amplifier — very useful on the stage.

Microphone Impedance
The 'impedance' of a microphone to alternating current varies greatly with its construction, and if its output is to be used to best advantage this impedance must match the input impedance of the amplifier.
    A ribbon microphone has very low impedance, usually a fraction of an ohm.
    Dynamic microphones usually have a low impedance of between 30 and 50 ohms.
    Crystal microphones and condenser microphones are high impedance devices. The impedance of the former is typically 5 megohms, that of the latter being 10–15 megohms.
    The input impedance of the modern transistor amplifier is generally low enough to accept the output of a dynamic microphone, though not of a ribbon microphone, which must therefore be used with a matching transformer.
    A high impedance microphone can generally be used satis-

factorily with a low impedance amplifier input, though the mismatch will cause some loss of effective sensitivity.

If a matching transformer is to be used the question arises as to where it will be fitted — at the microphone end or at the amplifier end of the connecting cable? The decision is easy to make because there is an important advantage in having a 'low' impedance line. A high impedance line (which means a line with an impedance in excess of 1000 ohms) is prone to pick up interference, such as mains hum, even when protected with a good earthed shield. The higher the impedance the greater the risk. High impedance lines must therefore be kept short, whereas shielded low impedance lines (having impedances below 250 ohms) can be long without risking hum pick-up.

In practical terms, a ribbon microphone will have a built-in transformer to give a line impedance of between 50 ohms and 250 ohms. A dynamic microphone will be used without a transformer. A condenser or crystal microphone will be used either with a short screened lead or with a built-in transformer which reduces the output impedance to 250 ohms or less. Where a low impedance line is used with a high impedance amplifier input, a matching transformer is fitted at the amplifier.

Microphone Pick-up Patterns
Standard microphones are operated by sound pressure waves acting on one side of the diaphragm. As pressure spreads through the air in all directions, pressure waves will affect such a diaphragm from whatever direction they arrive — even from behind. Standard microphones are therefore omni-directional in their pick-up.

The ribbon microphone has its diaphragm open to sound waves back and front, and being so light this ribbon moves with the air, vibrating in step with the sound pressure waves. It is therefore called a velocity microphone and picks up sound equally from in front of, or from behind the ribbon. A sound from one side causes the air to vibrate equally on each side of the ribbon and in a direction parallel to it. Sound from the side of a ribbon microphone is therefore picked up little or not at all. The pick-up pattern of such a microphone is, in fact, a figure of eight with maximum pick-up at right angles to the

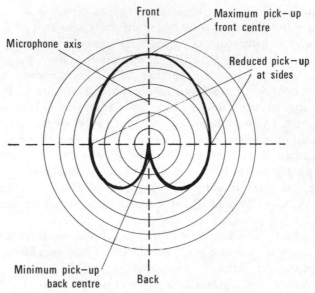

Fig. 30. Pick-up pattern of cardioid microphone

ribbon, front and back, the effect falling off steadily as the sound direction moves round, until there is virtually no pickup at right angles to the microphone's main axis.

There is a third microphone pick-up pattern, known as cardioid. This type of microphone picks up the maximum in front, the response falling away on each side until it reaches a minimum directly behind.

Any standard microphone can be converted to give a cardioid pick-up pattern by the acoustic design of its case. This allows some of the sound pressure waves to reach the back of the diaphragm. The design is such that front and back pressure act together in the case of sound from the front, and against each other, so cancelling out, in the case of sound waves from behind.

The Use of Microphones

We have examined the differences between sound perception by human beings and by the microphone, and we have reviewed the kinds of microphone available. There remains the question of which microphones to use, if there is a choice, and of how to get the best results.

For speech the most important consideration is clarity and

clarity is best achieved by picking up the maximum of direct sound and the minimum of reflected sound. The simplest way of achieving this, with any microphone, is to keep it close. Six to nine inches from the mouth is about right. The direct sound will be picked up quite loud, enabling the amplifier gain to be kept relatively low. Reflected sound is in any case much less loud, and with amplifier gain low it will not intrude. A foam shield over the mouth of the microphone will reduce breath noise.

The ribbon microphone, by cutting out much of the sound coming from each side, improves the ratio of direct to reflected sound and this type of microphone can be used further from the mouth. Eighteen inches is ideal, but any distance up to three feet should prove satisfactory. Incidentally the ribbon microphone is particularly useful for reading dramatic dialogue as one or more speakers can be located on each side. The effect of distance can also be achieved by a speaker remaining close, but speaking from the side of a ribbon microphone.

When using a good cardioid microphone speaker distance can be further increased up to six feet if necessary. Remember, though, that the angle of pick-up of these microphones is relatively small, and if a speaker moves much off the microphone's axis, even by turning his head to one side as he speaks, the pick-up will be reduced.

Recording Music
In the case of music somewhat different rules apply. Solo performers should be recorded as though they were speakers, only distances can be doubled. This is because reflected sound, or 'coloration' as it is also called, can enhance music as the listener is used to hearing it, and considers it normal provided it is not overdone.

A ribbon microphone gives the best result with ensembles and orchestras. This is mainly because of its practically weightless membrane which can respond instantaneously to the myriad of minute changes in the complicated waveform of such music. By placing a sound absorbent panel, such as acoustic tiling or celotex, behind such a microphone to reduce pick-up from the rear, this type of microphone can be used to effect at considerable distance from an orchestra. Used in this way its angle of pick-up will embrace a large orchestra.

Without the sound absorber behind, reflection from the rear of the hall would be over-emphasized when such a microphone is used so far back. Some expensive ribbon microphones are, in fact, built into a special case which gives them a cardioid pick-up. For music this is an ideal solution.

Standard cardioid microphones can be successfully used for orchestra pick-up, provided one takes into account their restricted angle of pick-up. Apart from keeping them well back, a procedure which their reduced pick-up from back and sides makes feasible, another solution is to use two such microphones together, directed with their main axes about 45° apart so as to give a wider combined field of pick-up. When this is done for mono recording it will, of course, be necessary to combine their electrical outputs by means of a mixer.

Recording in Stereo
There are three methods of placing microphones for stereo recording.

The first is to treat a pair of microphones as though they were ears, placing them about nine inches apart, facing at an angle left and right. In this case omni-directional microphones are unsuitable as they cannot discriminate between sounds from opposite sides. A pair of ribbon microphones or, preferably, cardioid microphones would be suitable for this arrangement. For recordings of speech, including dramatic dialogue, this system will give an excellent result. For reasons already explained in Chapter 4, this system will not usually give a really good stereo image when the recordings are of large ensembles or orchestras (Fig. 31).

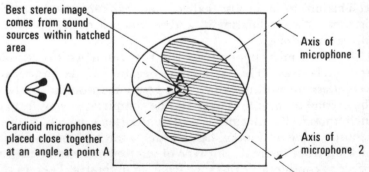

Best stereo image comes from sound sources within hatched area

A

Cardioid microphones placed close together at an angle, at point A

Axis of microphone 1

Axis of microphone 2

Fig. 31. Adjacent stereo microphones covering limited sound source

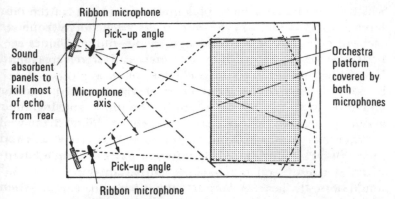

Fig. 32. Placing of stereo microphones for wide sound source

The second arrangement is to place the microphones well apart, a distance of between 2½m (8ft) and 4m (13ft) being suitable in most cases. Omni-directional microphones can be effectively used in this way, provided coloration by sound reflection is not allowed to become excessive. Sound absorbent panels (or heavy curtains) behind will help. Ceiling to floor reflections will be reduced if there is a good carpet (Fig. 32).

The use of ribbon microphones, placed well apart, will give fine orchestral recordings, but once again, sound reflection from surfaces close behind must be avoided.

Cardioid microphones are also entirely suitable for stereo recording with separated microphones. In this case, due to the restricted pick-up angle, the microphones would either have to be well back (and therefore even more widely separated), or used in pairs, as described in the previous section, so that the sound of the entire orchestra is picked up by each pair.

This brings us to the third method of stereo recording, in

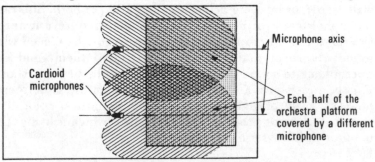

Fig. 33. Differential pick-up by stereo microphones

which the principle is not to pick up the same sounds from different positions and angles, but to use each microphone to pick up only part of a wide-based sound source. This is the basis of what the record manufacturers call 'stereo spectaculars'. When we listen to an orchestra, or to any other wide-based sound source, each ear hears all the sound, the stereo image being formed in the brain by the phase and loudness variations between the perception of each ear. (Fig. 33.)

When ribbon or cardioid microphones are placed so that each will pick up substantially different parts of a wide-based sound the result, on playback, is unlike anything a person would normally hear. A human cannot have one ear listening mainly to the first and second violins and woodwind, while the other ear hears principally the cellos, double basses, and brass. Directional microphones, on the other hand, can be used to achieve this effect. Clearly, however, such use will not produce a 'natural' stereo image, and while extreme separation has its place, it should be used with caution.

Studio Conditions
A great deal of experience and skill goes into the design and construction of recording studios. An announcement booth is usually made with highly sound absorbent walls, as reflective coloration reduces the clarity of speech. On the other hand music requires some, though not too much coloration.

For the amateur recordist the principles are clear. Bare rooms must be avoided. If one wall is bare the wall opposite must be made sound absorbent, whether it be with acoustic panelling, or by means of heavy curtains. Floor-to-ceiling reflection must be reduced either by having a thick wall-to-wall carpet, or by using acoustic ceiling tiles, or both. Substantial upholstered furniture will always help reduce unwanted reverberation. Microphones should preferably be placed with sound absorbent materials or walls behind them, and the microphone-to-sound source distance should be kept short. Finally, never have a loudspeaker monitor in the same room, however softly played. It will produce unnatural coloration even if it does not produce feedback howl, which is likely. For monitoring always use earphones.

The Choice of Equipment

Before a prospective buyer can choose tape-recording equipment he must know exactly what he wants to do with it. Will it be used only for entertainment? Or does he propose to attempt creative recording, such as the preparation of tape-slide programmes, recording sound effects for use in stage production, making sound tracks to accompany cine films, or making recordings of the local symphony orchestra and choir?

For entertainment pure and simple a cassette recorder can be more than adequate. These machines, whether mono or stereo, will give excellent results if well looked after. Cassettes are simple to load and unload and provided microphones are used intelligently, recording for fun is easy enough. An added advantage is that pre-recorded cassettes covering a wide range of music are available in the shops.

For the more demanding enthusiast who, nevertheless, does not wish to go in for a reel-to-reel recorder, cassette recorders are today available with the Dolby B noise reduction system built in. These machines will make excellent recordings and there is also a growing list of Dolby system pre-recorded cassettes available. Standard pre-recorded cassettes can, of course, also be played, as such recorders have a switch which cuts out the Dolby circuit.

Relatively inexpensive battery cassette recorders are available everywhere and are ideal for those who wish to make 'outside' recordings of animal noises, bird calls, out-of-door sound effects for use in dramatic productions or even to keep a record of a business meeting or conference.

For the more serious recordist, those for example who wish to collect the highest quality music on tape, or those who intend to do creative work which involves editing, a reel-to-reel tape recorder has advantages. A quality tape deck with Dolby system, played through a good high-fidelity audio set, can give results as good as any L.P. record. Were this not the case the record manufacturers would not make their master recordings on tape.

Two tape speeds, 9.5cm (3¾in.) and 19cm (7½in.) per second, are adequate for all normal purposes. If you wish to record long programmes the chosen machine should be able to accommodate 18cm (7in.) spools. Whether you need only a tape deck, which must be used in conjunction with a separate amplifier and loudspeaker, will depend on your specific need. If you have a mind to use your tape-recorder for outside recording, a machine with its own amplifiers and loudspeakers has the obvious advantage that you can immediately play back your recordings aloud for all those concerned to hear, as opposed to listening individually on earphones. The same is true when you give tape-slide shows or similar programmes outside your own home. In halls a separate amplifier may be necessary, but a tape-recorder with a good amplifier delivering between 3 and 8 watts of undistorted power will be found adequate for most purposes. Unfortunately, the variety of recorders on the market is today bewildering, and the best advice one can give is to decide one's precise need and one's budget limit, and then arrange for a supplier to demonstrate those recorders that do not exceed the price limit.

CHAPTER 7

Talking Pictures

One of the earliest systems used for motion picture sound was based on the disc. A 16in. lac disc was run at a relatively slow speed, the sound and picture being synchronized by means of a mechanical link between the film projector mechanism and the record turntable.

It was soon realized that the cumbersome mechanical system of synchronization could be avoided by having the sound track on the film itself. Fritz Pfleumer had anticipated this idea in his 1929 patent for coated tape. However, as film is used to produce pictures by passing light through it, it seemed logical to invent a system by which sound could be produced in much the same way.

Optical Sound Recording
The optical sound track used in motion pictures for many

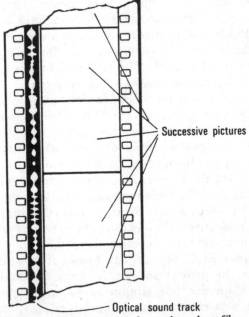

Fig. 34. Variable area optical sound track on film

years is of two kinds: variable area and variable density. While the recording mechanism is different, playback is carried out by identical units.

In both types of optical recording, the basic system consists of a beam of light which is focused to form a narrow horizontal strip of light which moves along a special light-sensitive track at one edge of the film. In the variable area system the length of the strip can be varied by means of a mirror galvanometer to which the audio signal is fed. As the galvanometer follows the audio waveform, the strip of light varies rapidly in length, producing a stripe of varying width on the film emulsion as it moves along.

In the case of variable density recording the light beam is modulated by means of a pair of vertically moving ribbons which act as a gate in the light path, varying the intensity of the light beam, and so the opacity of the stripe, which is of constant width.

Electro-mechanical systems are used in both cases to increase the signal-to-noise ratio.

Film speed for 35mm and 16mm sound recording is 24 frames per second. In the case of 35mm film, where each frame occupies 24mm along the film, a light band 0.05mm (0.002in.) wide will, in theory, record frequencies up to 9 kHz, which is the highest the system can handle. In practice a narrower light band is used. The actual light slot used is wider, the beam being focused down by a lens system.

The optical sound recording camera produces, as does the scene image, a negative on the film. This is processed in the usual way to produce a positive print which can be used directly in an optical projector, producing sound which is automatically synchronized with the action.

For playback the process is basically simple. A tiny beam of light is projected through the sound track at the edge of the film, passing on to a light sensitive cell. Originally a conventional photoelectric cell was used, but the newer solar cell is more efficient and is now commonly used.

The reader probably already knows that while a cinema film passes the projection gate in jerks, remaining momentarily still while the light shutter opens, moving on one frame each time it is closed, sound reproduction from an optical sound track depends on the film passing at constant speed.

This means that synchronized sound cannot be recorded on the film directly opposite the pictures to which it relates. In practice the sound is recorded 20 frames ahead of the picture on 35mm films and 26 frames ahead in the case of 16mm. After the film has passed the mechanism which caused it to move intermittently past the projection gate, it moves on to a flywheel stabilized sprocket to ensure constant speed as it passes the sound pick-up station. A similar system is used in the optical sound camera.

Magnetic Film Recording

When magnetic recording became well established and its advantages understood, it was natural that the motion picture industry should turn to this system.

The optical sound camera is rarely used today. Instead there are three systems of magnetic recording.

Both 35mm and 16mm film is available with a magnetic coating in place of a photographic emulsion. This type of recording film is used in a specially designed motion picture recorder. As the film is magnetically coated right across it can be used for multi-track recording. Some 35mm recorders use three tracks, each 5.4mm (0.2in.) wide. Alternatives are four track machines having 4mm (0.15in.) tracks, and six-track machines using 2.7mm (0.1in.) tracks. The 16mm magnetic film recorders use a similar system, but three tracks is the most accommodated on this film, and two is more common.

In order to secure synchronization both the camera and the recorder are driven by synchronous electric motors which are kept electronically interlocked with respect to speed. As the picture and sound film have identical sprocket holes, neither can slip and synchronization remains perfect.

The reason for having multiple tracks is to aid editing. Usually music is recorded on one track, sound effects on another, and dialogue on a third. Where two tracks are used the music and effects are recorded together and the dialogue on the second track. There are several reasons for sometimes using more than three tracks. Dialogue from different parts of a film set may be recorded separately. Overlapping sound effects may be put on separate tracks. Music may be recorded on two or three tracks to permit balancing during the editing process.

Magnetic film of this type is not used for projection. It is an editing aid, giving the sound engineer the facility of editing sound independently of picture editing. It makes it easy to control balance between music, effects and dialogue, and makes possible the dubbing in of separate dialogue takes (each separately synchronized) without disturbing the continuity of music or background sounds. It also makes possible the substitution of dialogue in one language with new dialogue in another, when a film is to be dubbed for a foreign market. In such cases the music and effects remain unaffected.

Once a master magnetic film has been edited the two or three sound tracks are combined and transferred to projection copies of the film. And since the projection equipment used in most cinemas is the well-established optical system, the final sound track is reproduced as a negative track which can be directly printed photographically on to the 'show' copies of the film.

Motion Picture Recording on Tape

Motion picture film is three times as thick as standard magnetic tape and the recorders that handle it are large and cumbersome. Magnetic film is also expensive. It was soon realized that if conventional $\frac{1}{4}$in. magnetic tape could be used for film work, the recorder would be smaller and more convenient, and the tape less expensive than film. The whole set up would be well suited to location filming because a magnetic tape recorder can be designed to be entirely portable. The only problem was that of ensuring perfect synchronization in the absence of identical sprocket holes on the media used to record picture and sound.

This problem was solved by building into the camera a device which produces a pulse which is recorded on a separate track on the tape. When the tape is played back the output of the pulse track is used as a control. A number of systems are used.

In professional work it is usual to re-record tape recordings on magnetic film before the editing process. The pulse track is used in this case to control the speed of the magnetic film recorder. If the camera used is designed to produce two pulses per picture frame, the tape recorder will automatically maintain a steady speed of 48 pulses per second on replay, the magnetic film recorder operating at 24 frames per second.

The pulse system has also been adapted to synchronize sound for 8mm films. In this case the camera is designed to produce 18 pulses each second (that is one for each picture frame when working at the standard speed of 18 frames per second) and these pulses are recorded on the lower half of cassette tape by means of a special cassette recorder which simultaneously records sound in mono on the upper half of the tape. With this system the cassette recorder is used for playback in conjunction with a special projector designed to maintain a projection speed of one picture frame for every pulse.

Direct Sound Recording

When complicated sound editing is not likely to be needed, as in filming for newsreels and TV news, the ideal system is direct magnetic recording on reversal film. For this purpose the film is supplied with a magnetic 'stripe' along one edge of the picture area. During exposure of the film the accompanying sound is recorded on the stripe. Because the film in the camera passes the gate intermittently, whereas for recording the stripe speed must be constant, the recording head is fitted below the gate and shutter assembly, so that the sound is recorded ahead of the picture frame to which it must synchronize. In the case of 35mm the recording head is 20 frames ahead, while in 16mm cameras it is 26 frames ahead.

On 35mm film the magnetic stripe is between the picture area and one row of sprocket holes, and there is a narrow

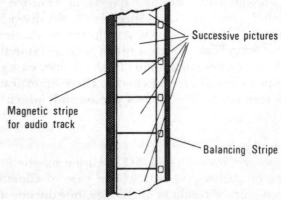

Fig. 35. Magnetic stripe on small gauge film

'balancing' stripe on the opposite edge, outside the sprocket holes. This is to provide the same thickness at each edge of the film, so as to ensure even spooling. On 16mm direct sound film one row of sprocket holes is omitted, the main magnetic stripe occupying the space where there is no longer a second row of holes. A narrow balancing stripe is accommodated beyond the sprocket holes on the opposite edge to the main stripe.

Nowadays 8mm direct sound cameras are rapidly becoming standard, and have the same stripe arrangement as 16mm film. In this case the recording head is 18 frames below the gate and shutter assembly.

Where direct sound is recorded, the stripe is unaffected by processing. As soon as development and reversal have been carried out the film is ready for use in a sound projector. While 35mm film for projection normally has an optical sound track (which can, of course, be made direct from a magnetic stripe film), TV film projection apparatus usually operates direct from magnetic stripe film. This saves time in the case of direct sound news films. It also means that special copies of feature films must be prepared with sound on magnetic stripe for TV broadcasting.

Modern TV projection apparatus not only uses magnetic stripe for sound, but dispenses with the shutter system used in optical projectors. Instead the film moves through the projector at a constant speed, each picture frame being scanned electronically to produce the signal required for TV broadcasting. Though TV frame speed in Europe is 25 frames/second, and film frame speed is 24, the discrepancy is too small for the viewer to notice. An electronic scanner is also available for 8mm film, which is made with a frame speed of either 18 or 24 frames per second. In the former case two TV frames (25 per second) are matched to three 8mm frames, so the film is scanned at $16\frac{2}{3}$ frames per second, which is near enough.

Wide Screen Systems
Cinemascope and 70mm Todd AO both use magnetic stripes for their accompanying sound. In the case of Cinemascope there are two pairs of tracks at each edge, one outside and one inside each row of sprocket holes. One inner track and the two

outermost tracks are used for three-speaker stereo sound, using one loudspeaker left, one centre and one right of the screen. The fourth track is used to provide 'surround' sound, the amplified signal being fed to an array of loudspeakers situated around the auditorium.

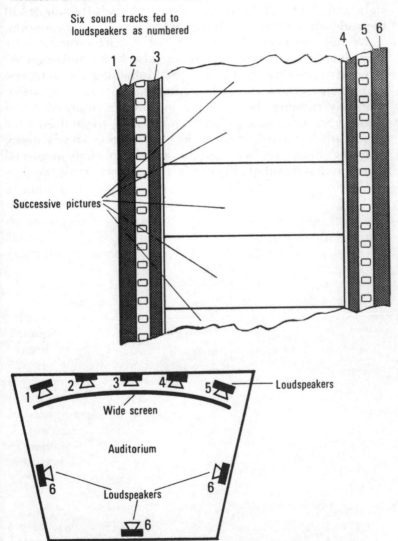

Fig. 36. Magnetic sound tracks on 70mm Todd AO Film and plan of loudspeaker distribution

In the case of 70mm Todd AO, the film accommodates six magnetic tracks, two on each of a pair of wide stripes on the outermost edges of the film, beyond the sprocket holes, two more being placed directly inside the holes. Five tracks are used for main stereo sound (left, inside left, centre, inside right and right), while the output of the sixth track is fed to the auditorium surround loudspeakers.

We have seen that 35mm films for cinema projection are reproduced with their optical soundtracks by normal negative-to-positive printing. In the case of films using the magnetic stripe system, show copies have their sound added by simultaneously running the master film with its recorded sound through an 'electronic printer' which takes a signal off each master track, recording it on the copy tracks. This is a long process as films have to be run through the machine at normal speed, so that sound quality can be constantly monitored.

CHAPTER 8

TV Pictures on Tape

John Logie Baird, the Scottish engineer who demonstrated the first practical television system, was also the first man to carry out 'video' recording. A plaque on the wall of a small restaurant in London's Soho district marks the place where Baird had a small 2nd floor laboratory and made the first video recordings on 78 rev/min gramophone records.

Baird's television system, first demonstrated in 1928, used the mechanical disc scanner (invented by Paul Nipkow in 1884) as opposed to the electronic scanner, the 'iconoscope', patented in the United States by the Russian emigrant, V. K. Zworykin, in 1925.

Being mechanical, Baird's scanner had very low 'definition'. The picture was divided horizontally into 30 lines (compare the 625 lines used today throughout Europe, and the 525 lines used in U.S.A.), the scan being completed 30 times a second. Baird's mechanical scanner had short lines and produced a video signal having frequencies ranging from zero (a blank screen) up to about 10 kHz. Though the latter was beyond the highest frequency that could be recorded on a gramophone record at the time, it was not very far beyond, and a typical signal from a Baird TV scanner, recorded in this way, could be played back through a Baird TV receiver, to give a picture only a little less detailed than if the signal had been passed by wire direct to the receiving scanner. It was a picture that was as good, and sometimes better, than when the signal had been broadcast and received before display.

The trouble with Baird's video recordings was not that they could not reproduce his video signals. The weakness lay in the lack of detail in the signals themselves.

Practical Problems

The principle of recording a television signal is no different from that used in recording sound. The practical problem today lies in the immense amount of detail in a typical video signal, detail which produces a waveform having a frequency range up to about 3.5 MHz. This high frequency waveform must be successfully recorded if that detail is to be retained in playback.

We have seen that the highest frequency that can be recorded on tape depends on two factors. One is the size of the magnetic gap in the recorder's record/replay head. The other is the time it takes for the individual particles in the tape coating to pass that gap, which in turn depends on the tape speed. With modern heads and the latest tape running at 38.1cm (15 inches) per second, the highest frequency that can be recorded and replayed effectively is in the region of 30 kHz. In order to record the frequencies of a modern TV signal, the tape speed would have to be increased to at least 12 metres (almost 500 inches) per second — a daunting proposition!

Early Video Tape Recorders
In fact this was the approach used in the design of early video tape recorders. In 1954 the Radio Corporation of America (RCA) built a recorder which used a tape speed of 360 inches per second. In theory this machine should have been able to record and replay a monochrome TV signal with reasonably acceptable definition. In practice it was a failure for several reasons. The bandwidth of an acceptable TV signal (that is the ratio between the lowest and highest frequency) is about 18 octaves (the frequency is doubled for each octave). It was found, however, that no tape recorder can cope with a bandwidth greater than 10 octaves. If the top frequency recorded effectively is the required 3.5 MHz, the machine's low frequency limit will be about 3,500 Hz, whereas an undistorted response down to about 15 Hz is needed to produce all the picture brightness variations met with.

Reducing the Bandwidth
Four years later the BBC in London attempted to solve this problem by dividing the video signal into two bands which were recorded separately on two parallel tracks. The upper band covered the frequencies from 100 kHz to 3 MHz, which is a range of about 5 octaves. The lower frequencies up to 100 kHz were modulated on to a 750 kHz carrier, producing a band of from 650 kHz (that is 750–100 kHz) to 850 kHz (750 + 100 kHz), which fell within the middle of the five octaves occupied by the upper frequencies, and could therefore be

easily recorded at the same tape speed. As the tape speed was too fast to accommodate the low audio frequencies, the accompanying sound had also to be modulated on to a high frequency carrier, so that it could be recorded simultaneously on the same tape. The BBC machine, called 'Vera' (Vision Electronic Recording Apparatus), had solved one of the main problems experienced on the earlier RCA recorder, but not the others. These were the problem of accommodating sufficient tape on a single spool for more than a few minutes of continuous recording, and the problem of controlling the high tape speed within fine limits. The first of these problems is self-evident. A modern 18cm (7in.) spool holding 540m (1,800ft) of $\frac{1}{4}$in. tape would be exhausted in less than $1\frac{1}{2}$ minutes when feeding tape at a speed of even 6.35m (250in.) per second.

As for accurate speed control of the tape, it was found that a timing error which put the tape ahead or behind its theoretically correct position much more than one millionth of a second would upset the synchronization of the lines on the TV screen. At high tape speed such accuracy was not easy to attain.

Transverse Recording
The breakthrough had been made in fact, in 1956, two years before 'Vera' was completed, by two American engineers. Charles P. Ginsburg and Charles E. Anderson, of the Ampex Corporation. They demonstrated a machine which used a 2in. wide tape travelling at slow speed while video heads mounted on a wheel rotated at right angles to the tape's direction of travel at a speed of 240 revolutions per second (where 50 Hz mains are used for power, the head assembly speed is 250 rev/sec; 240 remains the standard for 60 Hz mains). In this way the tape-to-head speed was high across the tape, though the latter moved slowly. As one head neared the edge of the tape, the next one on the wheel began to cross from the other edge, so that a continuous recording was made. The standard modern broadcast video tape recorder (VTR for short) has four heads on the tape scanning wheel, the system being known as 'quadruplex'. With the 2in. tape moving at 15 inches per second, a spool $12\frac{1}{2}$in. in diameter provides for 64 minutes of continuous recording.

The problem of bandwidth was simultaneously solved by frequency modulating the signal, before recording, in such a way as to reduce the bandwidth to a mere two octaves.

With the tape moving longitudinally at approximately 15 inches per second and the head assembly rotating across the tape at 250 (or 240) revolutions per second, the resulting magnetic scan on the 2in. wide tape used is a series of parallel tracks nearly, but not quite, at right angles to the tape, every fourth track being recorded by the same head as it comes round full circle. Each track is 0.01in. wide, adjacent tracks being spaced approximately half their width from each other. (The exact specification is for tracks to be centred 0.015625in. apart). Standard tape speed used on 50 Hz mains is 39.6875cm (15.625in.) a second, a speed of exactly 38.1cm (15in.) per second being used on 60 Hz mains.

Vacuum Guide

The reader may be wondering how a head moving around in a circle makes a track across a tape which, normally, is flat. Obviously this would be impossible. The answer is that the tape is moved across a vacuum assembly at the recording/playback station. The vacuum literally sucks the wide tape into a circular guide as it passes, so that it forms an arc of a circle of precisely the right radius (1.03315in. is standard). At the point where the heads make contact there is a small vertical depression in the vacuum guide exactly in line with the path of the heads, which allows the latter to press 0.003 inches 'into' the tape as they pass, ensuring perfect contact with the

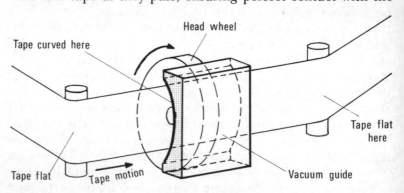

Fig. 37. Principle of VTR head wheel vacuum guide

coating. The curved portion of tape, from the last vertical guide past the vacuum guide to the next vertical guide, is known as the 'canoe'.

Transverse Tracks

The video signal is a scanning signal representing a number of horizontal lines. As the TV screen is scanned the scanning spot moves first along one line, then jumps back 'instantaneously' to the start of the second line, which it scans in turn. When it has scanned the entire screen the spot must make a bigger jump back to the start of the first line. In practice the spot first scans alternate lines, jumping back to scan those between, before the entire process is repeated. In the European 625 line system, the full process is repeated 25 times a second, referred to as 25 frames, but due to the system of interlacing alternate lines the screen is, in fact, covered by the scan 50 times a second; this is known technically as 50 fields. (In the USA the 525 line system has 60 fields, interlaced to produce 30 frames.)

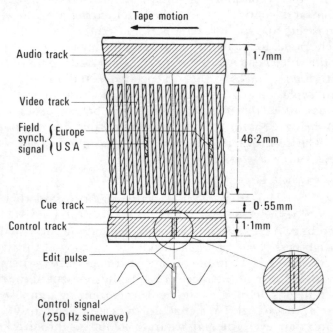

Fig. 38. Track layout on quadruplex VTR

Using the European system for our example, a little calcula-
tion will show that with the tape running at 39.6875cm
(15.625in.), and the picture at 25 frames per second, each
frame occupies 1.5875cm (0.625in.) along the tape, and is
made up of 40 parallel tracks. (In the USA each frame
occupies 0.5 inches (1.27cm), made up of 32 tracks. The
tracks in both systems have identical width and spacing.)

Longitudinal Tracks
As the continuous recorded TV signal occupies each track in
sequence, there has to be some provision for a smooth transition from each track to the next. This is achieved by overlapping. When the 2in. (5.08cm) tape is curved round the head
wheel it covers an arc of well over 90°. This provides a total
overlap of 0.38 inches (0.9652cm), or 0.19 inches (0.4826cm)
at each end of each track. While a 0.2in. overlap will be retained, part of the total overlap, top and bottom, will be
erased as the tape moves on, to provide space for longitudinal
tracks at each edge. The upper longitudinal 'audio' track is
used for the accompanying sound, and two lower tracks are
the 'cue' and 'control' tracks. The latter carries a signal which
controls the tape speed, and a periodic 'edit' pulse at the start
of each frame, to aid in frame location during tape editing.

As the video head wheel sweeps right across the path of these
longitudinal tracks, the associated audio and cue
record/replay heads are situated 'downstream' of the video
head assembly, the intervening distance between sound and
vision being 235mm (9.25in.), representing 0.6 seconds in
time. The control track head is placed as close to the video
head assembly as possible.

Speed Control
It must be clear from what has already been said that the
precision with which a VTR must operate is extremely
demanding. A clear detailed picture depends on the signal for
the brightness of each point on each line arriving at the screen
at precisely the right moment so that it is perfectly synchronized with the scan of the receiver. Only the moment of the start
of each field is defined by the field synchronizing signal which
is part of the actual TV signal. In the case of colour TV the
tolerances are even finer, if accurate colour synchronization is
to be maintained.

In the audio tape recorder there is only one speed control required, that of the tape transport. As long as this remains constant, and provided the tape record and playback speeds are reasonably close, the result will be acceptable. This is not the case with the VTR. In the first place the tape speed must not only be constant, but must be accurate. The slightest inaccuracy will put the transverse tracking of the video heads off their correct paths. In the second place the video heads themselves must track at exactly the correct speed. And thirdly each of the video heads must arrive at the edge of the tape at precisely the correct moment. Unless all these operations are perfectly timed the result will be a signal which will not synchronize with the picture tube scanning on TV receivers tuned to a broadcast from tape.

Servo Systems

There is only one method of achieving such great accuracy of movement of both the tape and of the head wheel. It is by means of highly sensitive automatic correction mechanisms known as servo systems.

While electronic servo systems can be complex, the principle is simple enough. The speed of rotation of any wheel can be monitored electronically by means of a tachometer which produces a predetermined number of electronic pulses per revolution. This series of 'output' pulses is next 'compared', again electronically, with a 'reference' series of pulses known to have the required frequency. Finally, the difference, if any, between the 'reference' pulse frequency and the 'output' pulse frequency is determined, once more by electronic means, to modify the speed of the motor and to reduce that difference, until the two frequencies are identical.

Record Mode Servo Action

Consider the head wheel of a European standard quadruplex VTR. The wheel must turn at 250 rev/sec. A tachometer designed to produce one pulse per revolution is fitted on the head wheel shaft. The signal produced should have a frequency of 250 Hz. As the VTR is to record a TV camera output, with which it must synchronize, the TV field signal, which occurs 50 times a second, is used as the control reference. This signal is passed through a five-times multiplier to produce a control pulse of 250 Hz.

The control pulse and head wheel tachometer pulse are fed into a comparator which produces a control signal that modifies the head wheel motor speed until the latter pulse synchronizes exactly with the former. Provided the tachometer pulse is designed to be made at the correct moment during the rotation of the heads, the head position on the tape will also synchronize with the TV signal so that the field synchronizing signal is always at the mid-point of a track. (We shall see shortly why this is necessary.)

The head wheel tachometer pulse is also fed to the capstan servo system. As the capstan revolves relatively slowly ($2\frac{1}{2}$ times a second is typical with a 6in. diameter non-pinch-roller capstan) its speed is monitored by an optical tachometer. This has a glass disc having a large number of black radial lines. Light passes through to a photo-cell which is used to 'read' the number of lines passing each second.

The capstan tachometer pulse is compared with a control pulse derived from the head wheel tachometer pulse to produce a control signal which modifies the speed of the capstan motor until the tachometer pulse rate matches the control signal pulse.

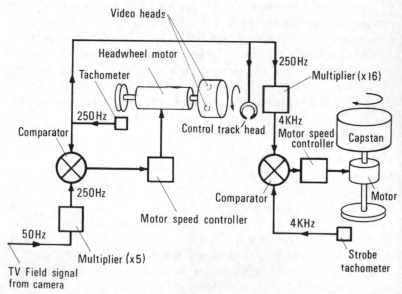

Fig. 39. Principle of servo system for record mode

During recording the head wheel tachometer pulse is simultaneously converted into a 250 Hz sine wave which is recorded on the control track of the tape, along with edit pulses derived from the field pulses of the original camera signal. (The edit pulse frequency varies. On some systems it is 25 Hz, on others 12.5 Hz).

Playback Mode Servo Action
In playback mode there is, of course, no camera field signal to serve as the head wheel servo reference. Instead the 50 Hz signal used in the studios to control the TV cameras is taken as the reference frequency. In a European broadcasting station this is an accurately maintained 50 Hz signal known as 'station sync'.

The same head wheel servo system is used for playback as for record, only in the former case the comparator is fed with the station sync instead of the camera field signals used in recording.

Once the head wheel speed has been established, the equipment must control the tape speed so that the heads, in turn, sweep across the tape precisely on the lines where the tracks have been recorded. Capstan speed is once again controlled by a servo system, only this time the control reference is the sine wave recorded on the control track of the tape. One adjustment remains. For while tape speed and head wheel speed are now both in synchronization, the sweep of the four heads may not be directly over the recorded tracks. To provide for lateral adjustment a variable electronic delay line is fitted between the control track output and the comparator input. The delay is adjusted until the output from the heads reads maximum on a meter.

VTR Electronics
We have seen already that signal processing for video recording and replay is considerably more complex than that used in audio recording. The technical details of these electronics go beyond the comprehension of the average non-technical reader, but the principles involved are not difficult to understand. In the record mode we start with the camera signal; this is fed to a frequency modulator circuit, the carrier normally lying between 3.5 and 8.5 MHz. The FM signal then passes to

an amplifier designed to feed the record heads so that the tape will be magnetized to saturation point on signal peaks. Equalization to compensate for head losses is carried out in the driver amplifier and the signal is fed into all four heads simultaneously, though modulation of the tape is only carried out by the heads in contact at any moment (one for most of the time; two during the overlap period).

Head Switching

During playback the main function of the electronics is to demodulate the FM signal read by the heads, to compensate for head losses by equalization, and to process the resulting video signal into a form suitable to feed to the radio transmitter. There is, however, one additional problem. If the output from each of the four heads were simply added, the signal-to-noise ratio would be unnecessarily low. This is because at any one moment only one head is reading a signal on the tape, though all four heads are contributing noise. To avoid this there has to be an electronic switching system and, as switching during the course of a picture line produces momentary interference, seen as a tiny 'spark', the switching has to be accurately controlled so that it takes place during the tiny time gap between consecutive lines. Once this has been achieved the VTR playback signal is to all intents and purposes identical with the recorded output signal which came from the director's control console at the TV studios and is ready for broadcasting, along with the accompanying sound signal, in the usual way. It is because of this head switching that it is necessary, as explained earlier, for the field synchronizing signal of a TV scan to be kept at the mid point of a track.

Feeding the Rotary Heads

There is another problem which applies equally to video recording and playback. This is the question of feeding signals to and from the heads mounted on a wheel rotating at high speed. Of course there can be no direct connection; instead the device used is a 'rotary' transformer. This is, simply, a transformer in which the secondary winding can rotate within the field created by the primary winding and its core. Design is such that the inductive coupling remains constant during rotation of the secondary winding. The rotary transformer of the quadruplex VTR is complicated by the need to feed the outputs of the four heads separately to the electronic switching circuit which connects only one head at a time during playback.

Editing Videotape

The convenience of editing recorded audio tape is as desirable, if not more so, in the field of video tape recording. While a programme recorded on tape will normally be directed, so far as possible, as a continuous live performance, there is always the possibility of errors which need to be removed before a recorded programme is broadcast. The inclusion of substitute material or new inserts, or for the assembly of recordings from various sources in the preparation of certain programmes, may also have to be considered.

Physical editing, by cutting the tape and butt jointing with the aid of thin adhesive tape is possible, but very time-consuming. If a splice is thus made without reference to the frame pulse the picture timing will be thrown out of synchronization and the new picture, after the splice, will start with the bottom edge of the scan somewhere in midscreen. The electronics will quickly correct the error and the picture will 'float' down to its correct position; but clearly this is undesirable. If track spacing is not maintained there will be a brief loss of picture, until the servo system brings the tracking back into line with the heads. A splice must therefore be made by cutting the two tapes each at the junction between two frames (as is done when splicing cine film) and along a line down the middle of the space between adjacent tracks. As the frames and tracks on tape cannot be seen a method of locating the edit pulse on the control track was developed. A suspension of fine iron carbonyl powder in a volatile liquid, is 'painted' along the control track. The iron is attracted to points of maximum magnetization, and when the liquid evaporates tiny clusters of the powder can be seen at each edit pulse. With this aid the tape can be accurately positioned in a splicing cutter, which will then cut the tape precisely between the two required tracks. When two tapes have been so cut, they can be butt jointed, using special pressure sensitive adhesive tape only 0.004in. thick to produce a serviceable splice which maintains track spacing and synchronization. A difficulty arises, however, over the sound track, which is 9.25in. ahead of the related video track. The only way of making a physical splice without the sound track altering 0.6 seconds late is to re-record and edit the sound tracks separately on audio tape, and then re-record back on to the spliced video tape in synchronization.

Electronic Editing
Videotape editing is today carried out by electronic means. What actually occurs is that a point is selected on a recorded tape A, at which a 'splice' is to be made to material B, from another VTR (or from another source such as a telecine output, or direct from a studio camera). An edit tone is recorded on the cue track of the tape at the appropriate point. When all is ready tape A is run in playback, and the material B, to be 'spliced' in, is run simultaneously with the frames of the two programmes synchronized. When the edit tone is picked up from the tape A cue track the VTR switches from playback to record at the instant of the following edit pulse. The signals from source B are recorded on tape A from this point on.

In practice there are a number of complications. As the erase head on a VTR is almost 9in. ahead of the head wheel assembly, the erase current has to be turned on exactly 0.6 seconds before the video heads are switched from playback to record. The audio head is switched simultaneously with the video heads. The switching of the erase and video heads must be highly accurate as this must not only occur between two consecutive lateral tracks on the tape, but between the same two tracks after the 0.6 second interval while the tape moves along.

While this procedure sounds complex it is, of course, achieved by electronic timing, and once the operator knows what is to be done electronic 'splicing' is relatively easy. As the edit tone on the control track is not a very precise cue in electronic terms, new and more accurate means have been evolved which define each individual frame on a video recording in the form of a binary address which can then be used as a cue which is read instantaneously by electronic means.

Care has to be taken to avoid errors in electronic splicing as when a 'splice' is made the original signal on the first tape is erased and a resplice can only be made at an earlier point. For this reason provision is now made for programmed 'practice' splicing, which transfers the monitor signal from the first to the second source without erasing and re-recording. When the operator is satisfied with the result seen on the monitor, the sequence can be reproduced from the 'programme' while the actual electronic 'splice' is made.

Video Cassettes
At TV stations which accept advertising, there is a need to broadcast a succession of short video recordings ranging from a few seconds to several minutes. And as the various advertisements are shown at various times and in differing sequences, a spliced set of advertisements would frequently have to be broken up and respliced, which is not feasible. Nor would there be time to play each advertisement from a separate spool. Tape threading and make-ready take too long.

The answer to this problem was solved by the invention of a special type of 'broadcast' cassette. Like the audio cassette it contains two spools, between which a length of tape remains fixed, and from which a loop of tape can be easily withdrawn. The broadcast cassette holds normal 2in. (5.08cm) video tape and is designed to fit on to a standard quadruplex VTR in place of open spools of tape. When a VTR broadcast cassette is fitted in position withdrawal of a loop of tape and its threading through the heads and capstan assembly is automatic, taking hardly six seconds. These cassettes, which are designed to play for a minimum of 2 seconds and up to a maximum of 6 minutes, fit into a carousel which can hold up to 24. They are fed alternately on to one of two mechanisms which carries them into position for playback. Using two VTRs a series of short advertisements can be played in sequence without a break. Start, synchronization and stop, including tape threading, rewind and unthreading, is controlled by cue track signals and is fully automatic.

CHAPTER 9

Video Recording in
Industry and the Home

The broadcast VTR is a remarkable combination of precision engineering and complex electronics. It is inevitably very expensive and its cost, while amply justified in television service, is generally beyond its worth as a tool for audio-visual communication in industry, let alone as a luxury for the home.

The idea of putting visual action on to tape, as an alternative to film, nevertheless holds many attractions. Independence from a processing laboratory is one; video recording can be played back immediately it has been recorded. The possibility of re-using tape is another; film, as well as its processing, costs money. Film cannot be re-used.

The electronics industry was well aware, when the basic problems of video recording had been solved, that there was a potential market for a smaller, less complex and less expensive system of video recording than that achieved with the broadcast VTR. Where there is a market, research will develop a product.

The first approach was to invent an alternative to the system of transverse scanning used in the quadruplex machine. The head wheel with its four heads, rotating at high speed, and the vacuum guide system of forming the wide tape into a 'canoe', with very fine dimensional tolerances, required engineering of a very high order, with consequent high cost. The invention of helical scanning provided the economic alternative required.

Helical Scanning
Imagine a tape wrapped around a cylinder; if the tape is at right angles to the axis of the cylinder, the two ends of the tape will be level with each other. If the angle between the tape and the cylinder's axis is adjusted, as in Figure 40, the tape coming round the cylinder can be made to pass just above the ongoing tape. The tape circling the cylinder is in contact all round, but its 'circle' is slightly skew, forming what is known as a 'helix'. If the cylinder is now rotated, a point 'A' on its surface under the top edge of the oncoming tape will travel round under the tape, crossing it at an angle, until it again reaches point 'A' at

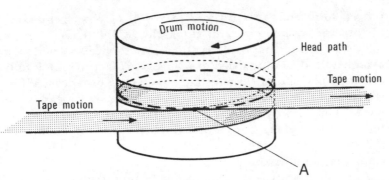

Fig. 40. Tape path for helical scanning

the bottom edge of the outgoing tape, where the latter touches the top edge of the oncoming tape. If, before the cylinder rotates a second time, the tape is moved forward a fraction, passing around the cylinder, the point 'A' will now be in a position to trace a second path on the underside of the tape parallel and close to the first. If, finally, instead of moving the tape abruptly forward each time point 'A' on the cylinder returns to the adjacent edges of the tape, the tape is moved forward slowly but steadily, the rotating spot 'A', will scan a series of close parallel tracks on the tape. By substituting a record/replay head for point 'A' on the cylinder, we have all the elements required of a video tape scanning system.

In practice, to give a typical example, using a tape speed of 19.1cm (7½in.)/sec., and a cylinder of 76mm (3in.) diameter, the cylinder would have to rotate at a little over 50 rev/sec to achieve a head-to-tape speed of 500 inches/second, and with a 360° helical 'wrap' only one head would be needed. Each diagonal track would be just under 240mm (9.6in.) long, from tape edge to tape edge.

This clearly implies a considerable saving in tape and a simplification of the mechanics. The ½in. (1.27cm) tape travelling at 7½in./sec (19.05cm) will replace 2in. (5.08cm) tape travelling at 15in./sec (38.1cm/sec), one head will replace four, and a drum scanner speed of 50 rev/sec will provide the required tape-to-head speed. With all these 'savings' there must be a corresponding 'loss'. This appears in two forms. First there is a reduced track width to about half the broadcast VTR standard, which implies a lower output. Fortunately this has

proved sufficient to record and play a picture perfectly satisfactory for commercial and domestic CCTV (closed circuit
television) use as opposed to broadcast service. Second, the
assumed head-to-tape speed of 500in./sec (12.7m/sec), is only
about 30 per cent of the speed achieved on a broadcast VTR,
which is 1620in./sec (41.148m/sec) on the European standard. This slower 'writing' speed (as it is called) implies
reduced definition, but here again, a speed of 500in./sec
(12.7m/sec) has proved generally adequate for CCTV use in
commerce and the home.

As we shall see, the use of only one head instead of four pre-
sents practical difficulties and most CCTV recorders have two
heads on the scanning drum. One head can be used, however,
provided a narrowing of the TV picture by the loss of some
lines at the top or bottom is accepted. The absence of the
vacuum guide and the substitution of a relatively slow rotating
drum for the high speed quadruplex head wheel makes for
significant economies in the mechanical engineering involved
in manufacture. Above all the tape saving is considerable. In
our example the CCTV recorder uses one eighth of the tape
area required to run a broadcast VTR for a given period of
time.

Practical Helical Scanners
The reason why one head is impractical on a drum scanner is
simply because there is bound to be a loss of signal, however
slight, at the point where the head crosses from the lower to
the upper tape. In theory there need be no loss of signal if the
entire width of the tape were used, and the upper edge of the
incoming tape exactly touched the lower edge at the point
where it left the drum. But there would then be no spare tape
for longitudinal sound and control tracks, which are both
essential. Provided the loss of a few lines, top and bottom of
the picture scan, is accepted, the narrow bands required for
audio and control tracks, along each edge of the tape, can be
erased after recording the video signal and then used for the
two new tracks.

This type of tape format around a cylinder is called the
Alpha Wrap, because the tape path resembles the Greek letter
α. To achieve full picture width scanning, the Alpha Wrap is
modified by allowing the tape to keep contact with the drum

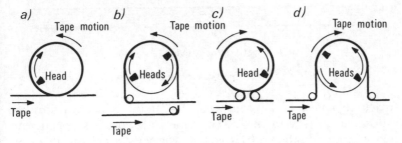

Fig. 41. Alternative helical scanning systems

for only a little over 180°, and by using a pair of heads which make contact alternately.

An alternative format used in CCTV recorders is the Omega Wrap, in which the tape path resembles the Greek letter Ω. As the tape path is still a helix, the only real difference is that the direction of the incoming and outgoing tape is altered by running it around short radius guides. As the tape does not cross itself the helix can be adjusted so that the upper edge of the incoming tape overlaps the lower edge of the outgoing tape, to provide space for audio and control tracks. This does not, however, obviate the loss of lines at the picture's edge as this wrap cannot cover the complete 360° of the drum, since the guides occupy some space.

In all the formats shown in Figure 41 the tape rises in a helix from the point it arrives at the drum until it leaves it. Tapering tape guides achieve this when the drum axis is at right angles to the main tape direction. The diagrams show the head drums rotating in the opposite direction to the tape motion. This is not essential, but it has the advantage of achieving the maximum head-to-tape speed, by adding the tape speed to the drum speed.

Helical Scanning Track Format

Due to the helical system of scanning the track layout on this type of video recorder is very different from that of the broadcast VTR. While the longitudinal tracks are retained at the edges of the tape, the video tracks cross the tape at an acute angle; this video track angle lies typically, between 3° and 5° to the edge of the tape.

As each video track is much longer than on the broadcast VTR, it is convenient on helical scanning machines for each

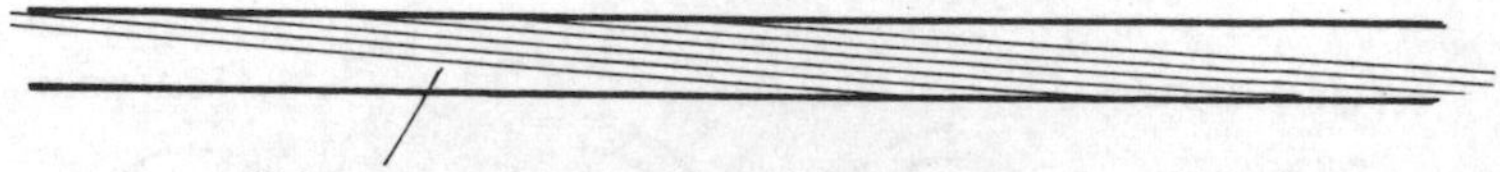

Video track format (5 tracks shown)

Fig. 42. Video cassette track format

track to contain one complete TV field. This provides an added advantage in that if the tape transport is stopped, the drum scanner will continue to scan the same track on the tape, thus providing 'stop' motion. If the tape moves at less or more than its correct speed, a slow or fast motion scan can be achieved, provided the ends of each individual TV scanning line on one track line up with the ends of those on adjacent tracks. This is necessary because the altered tape speed results in a difference between the head tracking angle and the angle of the tracks, so that the head will cross slowly from one track to the next. As the head is wider than the unrecorded 'guard' band between adjacent tracks, the picture will remain established if the beginning and end of each scanning line on adjacent tracks present themselves to the head at the same moment. Most helical scan recorders are designed to ensure that this is so. When the head crosses the guard band a horizontal 'noise' band floats vertically across the picture, but this is a small price to pay for the bonus of variable-speed slow motion on playback. There will, of course, be a stationary noise band when the tape movement is stopped, but this can be conveniently adjusted to remain near the top or the bottom of the TV screen.

Speed Control

Servo systems used on sub-standard video recorders are similar in principle to those used on the broadcast VTR, though in general they are less complex. When recording from camera the camera field synchronizing signal is the basis of drum scanner speed control, and the equivalent field synchronizing signal serves the same purpose when recording a TV programme from a receiver. A control track is also recorded to provide playback synchronization. While capstan speed may also be controlled by a servo system using the drum scanner tachometer pulse as its reference, a less expensive expedient is to drive the capstan from a synchronous AC motor, relying on the stability of the AC mains frequency to maintain the correct tape transport speed. On machines providing a slow and stop motion facility, a variable capstan speed, independent of the drum scanner speed, will in any case be necessary on playback.

Electronics
The electronics of the sub-standard video recorder are similar in general concept to those of the broadcast VTR. Any input signal at normal video frequency must have its bandwidth reduced by modulation before it can be recorded on tape, and the playback output must be demodulated and equalized before it can be fed to a TV picture tube. As the domestic TV receiver is designed to carry out demodulation of an FM signal, many sub-standard video recorders are designed to produce an equalized FM output which can be fed direct into the aerial socket of a conventional TV receiver. All that is necessary is for one of the TV set's unused channels to be tuned to the carrier frequency of the recorder. The TV set can then receive the signal, demodulate it, amplify it, display the video on the picture tube and process the audio in the usual way. It might be thought that incoming TV signals could be recorded directly on tape after suitable amplification; but as the video recorder must operate on an unused channel frequency for playback without interference to be possible, it is, in fact, necessary to demodulate an incoming TV programme signal

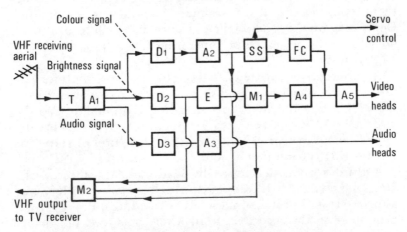

Fig. 43. Principle of typical video cassette recording system

and then remodulate it before recording. In any case, a recorder without its own frequency modulation circuit would be unable to accept a TV camera output.

Open Reel Formats

There is a large number of open-reel substandard VTRs on the market, and while no agreed standards have emerged, the most commonly used tape is 2.54cm (1in.) on a 20.32cm (8in.) spool, though the use of 1.27cm ($\frac{1}{2}$in.) tape is also fairly common. All employ helical scanning systems with either one or two video heads, and tape speed varies from 12.7cm (5in.) per second, to 29.2cm (11.5in.) per second. A widely used tape speed in Europe is 17.19cm (6.77in.) per second and in America 24cm (9.45in.) per second. These apparently odd speeds have been chosen because they provide maximum tape economy consistent with an acceptable minimum track spacing, while matching the local TV and AC current standards to the helical/scan format.

Cassette Systems

The obvious advantages of the cassette for the non-expert user was bound to lead to the design of the video cassette recorder (VCR for short), and four very different systems have appeared on the market. Philips, using 1.27cm ($\frac{1}{2}$in.) tape, make a cassette 14.4 × 12.7 × 4.1cm, in which a pair of spools are stacked vertically one above the other. Tape threading on their twin-headed drum-scanner recorder is automatic. Depending on the tape thickness the cassette will record up to 60 minutes, the machine operating at a tape speed of 14.29cm/sec.

An alternative cassette system, pioneered by Sony, uses $\frac{3}{4}$in. tape on twin spools mounted side by side in a cassette measuring 22.1 × 14 × 3.3cm. Tape threading is automatic and the associated VCR is a twin-headed drum scanner machine designed for a tape speed of 9.53cm/sec. Cassettes of thin tape provide up to 60 minutes of continuous recording.

A third system, developed by National (Matsushita) uses $\frac{1}{2}$in. tape on a 13 × 12.8 × 2.9cm single spool cartridge. The associated VCR provides automatic threading on to a permanent spool in the recorder, from which it is rewound before removal of the cassette. The machine operates at a tape speed of 16.322cm/sec, and provides 36 minutes of continuous recording.

Finally, IVC manufacture a VCR which uses 1in. tape on a standard 20.32cm (8in.) NAB reel fitted in a cartridge which provides automatic threading. Tape speed is 17.19cm (6.77in.)/sec and recording time 60 minutes. The tape system provides compatibility with a number of open-reel European machines.

Choice of Video Recording Equipment

The choice of a substandard video recorder depends very largely on the purpose for which it is wanted. The facility of cassette loading is an undoubted advantage, and with 60-minute cassettes now available it would be unwise for the amateur recordist to go in for a reel-to-reel machine, especially as the latest VCRs provide editing facilities. Unless one is interested in spending a great deal of money the choice today is limited, though new machines are likely to become available during 1978.

For the amateur who wishes to record in colour at home at minimum cost the obvious choice is the Philips N 1502 with its built-in TV tuner and clock, which will switch on the machine to record a programme while you are away. Output is suitable for connection to the aerial socket of a normal colour television. The price of the latest model is around £600.

For commercial or educational work, where the buyer is prepared to pay more for improved performance, the Sony VO 1810 colour VCR, at just under £1000, is a good buy. A tuner for TV programmes is an extra, the machine's normal input being for signals at video frequency. Output is suitable for connection to a normal colour TV.

TV cameras suitable for use with a VCR vary enormously in price. The cheapest modern colour camera from Japan sells at a little over £2000. On the other hand Hitachi sell a monochrome TV camera for under £150.

Reproduction of Video Tapes

Pre-recorded audio tapes are manufactured by the process of playback of the master tape and simultaneous re-recording on a bank of connected recorders. The process can be carried out at higher-than-normal tape speed, but is considerably more expensive than the stamping of gramophone records.

The copying of video-tapes by this process becomes prohibitively expensive if more than one or two duplicates are wanted, and two new rapid processes have been developed using high energy chromium dioxide tape.

In both processes the copies are made by face-to-face contact with the master tape. As this produces a 'mirror' image the master must itself be a mirror image of the required format so that the copies can be played back on standard machines.

In one process the master recording is made on high-output chromium dioxide tape by means of a modified VTR designed to record in the required mirror-image format. To produce copies the master tape is now pressed face-to-face in contact with a standard ferric oxide tape and passed through a low frequency alternating field. This system produces an almost perfect 'positive' copy of the original, though its output is somewhat less than an original recording on standard tape. While the process is efficient at the high video signal frequencies, losses are considerable at low frequencies and the longitudinal tracks have to be re-recorded by conventional means. However the system is rapid, as the paired tapes can be passed through

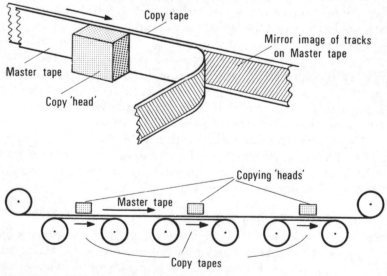

Fig. 44. Principle of video tape contact copying

the AC field at speed, a one hour programme being copied in about six minutes. Machines are available to make five copies from one pass of the master.

The alternative system does not require the original to be recorded in mirror format, but produces a mirror inter-copy on chromium dioxide tape, and the duplicates also on this high energy tape. The 'thermal' system, as it is called, relies on the fact that the magnetic properties of tape coatings are lost by heating. The new chromium dioxide tape is raised to its critical temperature of 125°C, placed in face-to-face contact with the standard tape master, and quickly cooled. The result is a mirror print of the master on the new tape. Moreover it is a print with higher magnetic energy than the original. The process is now repeated, using the chromium-dioxide mirror inter-copy as the master. The new tape is heated to 125°C, placed in contact with the inter-copy, and rapidly cooled as soon as contact is made. The result is a positive copy almost as good as the original ferric oxide master. It has a lower energy than the inter-copy, but its output is still higher than that of the original.

The critical temperature of ferric oxide is higher than that of chromium dioxide, so there is no danger of losing the magnetic signal on the master. Care must be taken, however, to ensure that the inter-copy coating does not quite reach 125°C, while the final copy coating temperature does. Otherwise the inter-copy signal would be lost.

CHAPTER 10

New Ideas for Today and Tomorrow

When John Baird made video recordings on 78 rev/min records in 1927 he was anticipating, by over 40 years, non-magnetic systems of video-recording which are being developed today. Before we examine the Teldec and Philips video disc systems it seems logical to describe the magnetic disc recorder already widely used on television. This is the machine used frequently on sports programmes for 'action replays'.

The Action Replay Recorder
The basis of this system, which was pioneered by the Ampex Corporation, is a heavy 40.64cm (16in.) diameter metal disc with a magnetic surface. A copper coated aluminium disc is manufactured and polished so that its two faces are level to within 1 thousandth of a millimetre (4 millionths of an inch). A thin layer of magnetic nickel cobalt alloy is laid on this non-magnetic base and given a coating of rhodium only a few millionths of an inch thick. The coating protects the nickel-cobalt, prevents surface corrosion and takes a very high polish. The disc weighs about $2\frac{1}{2}$ kg ($5\frac{1}{2}$ lb).

The disc is rotated at TV field rate (50 rev/sec in Europe) by a servo-controlled motor and specially designed heads are placed in contact to produce circular magnetic tracks spaced at 0.01in. (0.254mm) centres, including a 0.00635in. (0.16129mm) guard band. With this spacing there are 100

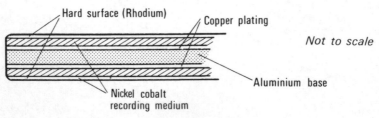

Fig. 45. Section of magnetic video disc

concentric tracks to the inch (2.5cm) and, with the outer 4.5 inches (11.43cm) in use, each side of the disc accommodates 450 tracks. With the disc rotating at 50 rev/second, the outer track will travel at 2570 inches/second (65.278m/sec), the innermost at 1100 inches/second (27.04m/sec) — sufficient for magnetically recording a colour TV signal. As the field frequency of European TV is 50 per second, exactly one field per revolution can be recorded on such a disc rotating 50 times a second, and if the tracks are concentric circles (as opposed to one continuous spiral) a stationary playback head will reproduce the same frame 50 times a second, producing a still picture.

To obtain continuous motion there are two heads. When one revolution is complete the recording signal is transferred to the second head, aligned over the adjacent track, and while this track is being recorded the first head moves across, ready to receive the signal when the second track has been recorded. By this 'leap frog' action the TV signal is recorded, field by field, on separate concentric tracks. In order to avoid the necessity of the heads having to 'jump' back eventually from the inner to the outermost track, the heads record every other track on their first pass, thus reaching the innermost after 25 revolutions; they then start moving outwards again, recording on the alternate tracks, until they arrive once again at the last but one outer track. The 450 available tracks on one side of the disc are covered in 9 seconds. The underside of the disc is used with two more heads timed to take over immediately after the 9 second sequence is complete. In this way one disc can carry 18 seconds of continuous action.

On playback the alternate tracks, first inwards and then outwards, are followed as before. Now, as each track is a circle containing a complete field, every pair of alternate tracks carries one complete interlaced TV frame, and by playing back from the same pair of tracks continuously a perfect still picture can be obtained. By arranging for the heads to play each track twice before 'leapfrogging', slow motion is obtained, the action taking twice as long. Even slower action by repeating frames more than twice between head movements, and 'fast' motion is also possible. As a complete frame lasts 1/25 second, the machines are designed to 'freeze' the action, if necessary, to 1/50 second, by playing back the same field continuously, transferring every other one to the alternate interlaced lines in the TV signal. Reverse action is also possible.

Although 18 seconds is not long, it has been found sufficient in sport for the kind of action replay that is needed. In practice the recording machine has two discs, each with four heads. When in use the operating disc always holds the last 18 seconds of action, but no more, as the previous action is erased as new action is recorded. To enable a sports editor to keep any sequence for action replay, the machine can be switched instantly to the second disc, and during the following 18 seconds the action recorded on the first disc is played back and can be broadcast as an immediate action replay (in normal or slow motion) while the continuing live action is stored temporarily on the second disc. During playback the replay signal can, of course, be simultaneously re-recorded for retention.

Mechanical Video Recording

The advantages of disc over tape have led to a number of other developments intended to provide video recordings which can be produced cheaply in large numbers for the general public. Two systems, which were first demonstrated successfully several years ago, deserve mention.

The Teldec system developed together by Telefunken and Decca employs a thin flexible disc carrying microgrooves so fine that 25 of them occupy the space of a single groove on a normal L.P. record today. Revolving at 25 rev/sec in Europe (30 rev/sec in USA) each groove carries the waveform required for one standard 625 line TV frame, comprised of two interlaced fields. The signal is frequency modulated before hill-and-dale recording; this ensures a groove of fixed width and undulations of fixed amplitude, the only variable being the frequency.

As no conventional mechanical stylus could follow undulations of well over a million cycles per second without physical damage either to itself or to the record groove, an entirely new idea was devised and successfully developed. The stylus is a tiny knife edge which slides along the groove. Being longer than the distance between the waveform 'peaks' of the lowest frequency recorded it is borne at all times by two or more successive peaks, and since these are at constant amplitude, it does not vibrate at all.

The signal is detected, not in terms of movement, but as pressure variations. Each 'peak' in the groove exerts pressure on the knife edge and the pressure changes are 'read' by the sensitive peizo-electric element on which it is mounted. The resulting signal is demodulated and processed electronically into the form required for picture display on a TV picture tube.

As the groove is too fine for the light stylus to follow it un-aided, the latter is drawn across the disc mechanically, as is done in audio disc-cutting. And to ensure constant pressure between the disc and the stylus, the disc is supported by a thin air cushion, formed by blowing compressed air through holes towards the centre of the servo-controlled turntable.

The system, which has produced good quality colour pictures, is a reproduction system only so far as the consumer is concerned. Recording is complicated and is carried out from film at a reduced action speed. Once the master disc has been successfully cut the production of copies is carried out by normal stamping techniques and is correspondingly cheap. An 8-inch disc will 'play' for 5 minutes, and a 12-inch disc for approximately a quarter of an hour. Teldec equipment and recordings have been on sale in Germany since 1966.

Optical Video Recording
An alternative approach, still under development by Philips and MCA of the United States, eliminates the physical stylus altogether, replacing it by a light beam which 'reads' depressions on the disc. These shallow elongated 'pits' follow a spiral path of roughly the same pitch as the microscopic Teldec groove and there is no continuous physical groove. The disc, pressed in vinyl by conventional methods, is plated with a thin, highly reflective aluminium layer. It revolves at TV frame speed (25 rev/sec in Europe, 30 rev/sec in U.S.A.), producing one complete frame of two interlaced TV fields for each revolution. The spot of light which 'reads' the depressions (audio, colour and video detail are all suitably modulated and combined in a single signal) is produced by a small laser and is only 0.001mm in diameter. This light spot is reflected from the surface of the aluminium disc coating into a photo-diode, and due to the refraction caused as the spot runs along each

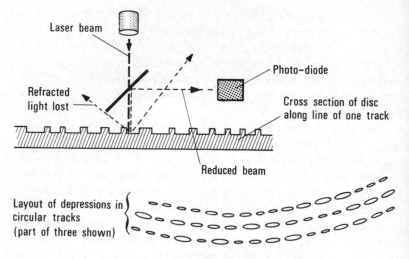

Fig. 46. Principle of optical video disc

narrow depression the output of the photo-diode varies, producing a signal suitable for processing.

Recording is achieved at video speed, using a glass disc coated with a photo-sensitive emulsion exposed to a laser light spot. Exposure and development of the disc is followed by an etching process which produces a master which can immediately be played, or used for pressing a negative and then positive copies by current audio disc techniques.

The optical playback system was chosen, say Philips, as it results in a disc which suffers no wear and which, if kept clean, will last indefinitely. A 12in. Philips/MCA optical videodisc will 'play' for approximately 30 minutes. The system has an advantage over the mechanical system in that the spiral track of the laser 'pick-up' can be triggered electronically to jump back a track either once per revolution of the disc (producing a still picture) or at preselected intervals (resulting in slow motion). The jump is made during the minute interval between successive frames. The audio signal will, of course, become unintelligible when the recording is used in this way.

In theory the still picture mode can be used to store individual pictures, instead of a motion series; in this case a single 12in. disc could act as a library of well over 50,000 different colour photographs which, by means of a built-in digital address system, could be individually selected and displayed on a TV picture tube.

Other Video Systems

There are other systems of recording and reproducing motion pictures, either in existence or under development; but as these are, in reality, extensions of the conventional motion picture film system, using electronic scanning instead of intermittent frame optical projection, they do not constitute video recording in the accepted sense of storage of a continuous electronic waveform. Such systems have been well documented and as the reader will find descriptions available in other books, I do not propose to explain or evaluate them here. Even the two video disc systems I have described have a future as yet uncertain in terms of public acceptance. The relatively inexpensive Video Cassette Recorder is a reality which provides the owner with recording as well as the playback facility. Already well established the VCR has clearly come to stay.

Recording and Copyright

The basis of the law of copyright is the financial protection of the authors of literary and dramatic works, and of the composers of music. The sources of income are various and include the sale of published written material and music, the sale of recordings of music and readings, the sale of films and video recordings of dramatic performances and literary presentations, the proceeds of live public performances of music, dramatic works and literary presentations, the proceeds of public presentations of sound recordings, films and video recordings, and the proceeds of radio and television broadcasting of written material, music and dramatic presentations.

The system of financial protection is based on defining the ownership of copyright and the prohibition of reproduction or presentation of such material for gain without the permission of the copyright owner; such permission is usually granted in return for an agreed fee.

Copyright ownership is vested not only in the original author or composer, but separately in those who, having obtained permission, rewrite original works (film scriptwriters and musical arrangers are typical examples). Copyright also exists separately in recorded performances of all kinds, whether on disc, tape or film. And a further copyright exists in the broadcasting (either sound or television) of any programme material.

The provisions of the law of copyright that concern the manufacture and sale of gramophone records, video discs, and recorded audio and video tapes are well known to those concerned professionally. The law concerning the amateur recordist is, however, not so widely understood and is not infrequently infringed.

For example it is an infringement of copyright to re-record any professional recording without permission of all the copyright owners concerned, whether for public or private replay, even when no financial gain is involved. So every time you borrow an L.P. from your neighbour and record it without permission on a cassette or on a home movie sound track you are breaking the law. The reason is simple; by so doing you are obtaining a copy of a performance of a copyright work without paying any fee to the record manufacturer, the performers, the musical arranger or the composer, all of whom would receive a share of the price of a new disc. All professional recordings are subject to copyright law, though general permission to copy may be granted by the owner. Such is the case with the B.B.C. 'Sound Effects' series of L.P.s, which bear a sleeve note which reads: 'Despite the prohibition notice on the label, the copying of the Sound Effects in this record on to tape for use in conjunction with a play, or dubbing on to film, is permitted.'

Recording of radio or television programmes is possible, however, without infringing copyright, provided the recording is made for private purposes only, and provided no other copyright is infringed. Unfortunately it is all too easy to infringe other copyrights. Recording of a broadcast gramophone record would be an infringement of the law for exactly the same reason as explained in the previous paragraph. On the other hand, a private recording of a B.B.C. documentary programme prepared specially for television would not normally constitute an infringement, because such a programme is intended for viewing in the home, and a private recording replayed later in the home would not be depriving the writer, presenter, technicians or others involved of any financial gain.

Whether a private recording of a play produced specially for television constitutes an infringement of copyright will depend on the agreement between the TV company and the author (who holds the original copyright), and on the use of any other copyright material (such as music) in the production. In general it is not considered an infringement to record radio and television programmes, other than professionally recorded material available for general sale in the shops, provided such recordings are made for private use only and are never replayed in public.

INDEX